Send Us A Minister . . .

any minister will do

by
Walter L. Cook

A Courier of Maine Book
One Park Drive
Rockland, Maine 04841

Library of Congress Card Catalog Number: 78-53942

International Standard Book Number: 0-913954-31-4

A Courier of Maine Book

Courier of Maine Books are published by
Courier-Gazette, Inc.

Printed in the United States of America

To Fred Whittaker,
President of Bangor Theological Seminary.
From 1940 to 1942,
student pastor at Robbinston and Red Beach.

Preface

The hundreds of little churches dotting our country-side are a settled part of the contemporary Maine scene.

Along with the grange hall, the general store, the volunteer fire house, the town hall, stands the village meeting house often set on a bleak hillside, painted white, with green shutters and window panes of clear glass cut eight by ten.

For over twenty years I have driven the main roads and side roads of the state visiting many of these churches to inquire about the work being done in them by student ministers from the Bangor Theological Seminary.

During these years I have kept a diary in which I have recorded the experiences of the young parsons as they served their first parishes. What follows is a gallery of glimpses that exhibits a patience on the part of church people with these fledgling ministers that has inspired my gratitude and wonder.

The same gallery also displays a dedication on the part of many student pastors that has made my task as the Seminary's field education director a rewarding and sometimes exciting vocation.

Introduction

"Send us a minister, any minister will do."

This request came recently to the Field Education Office of the Bangor Theological Seminary from a Maine church far to the north near the Canadian border.

"Any minister will do"! Surely a church should be more selective when asking for a pastor.

Although the request sounds heartbreakingly casual it is really a cry of desperation because it is almost impossible for some small churches in Maine's isolated villages to get a minister, any kind of minister.

When a Methodist, Congregational, or Baptist Church in some remote community of Maine loses its minister it turns to Conference or Convention headquarters for advice about his replacement. The officials of these denominations do all they can to help a church in its quest for a new pastor, providing lists of ministers who may be available and are agreeable to a change of pastorate, furnishing data about these ministers, and suggesting procedures for getting in touch with them.

But for many churches in out-of-the-way hamlets and towns of Maine, denominational officials seldom know of candidates to suggest. There is no queue of ministers panting to serve in churches in Magalloway or The Forks or Meddybemps. These churches are far from city centers, and can pay, even with denominational assistance, only a meager salary. For this reason a Methodist district superintendent or Congregational Conference minister or Baptist general secretary may be unable to suggest the name of a single ordained clergyman who will consider moving to one of these tiny wilderness churches.

Ministerial supply is a problem not only to churches in rural Maine, but also to congregations suffering from budget limitations in some of the state's larger towns and even cities. Many of these cannot adequately support a full-time minister.

"Send us a minister, any minister will do" is indeed a cry of despair. The church member who wrote that sentence in a letter to me lives in a hamlet seventy-five miles from the nearest city. He knew that no capable fully trained minister with a wife, and children to educate would come to serve a church that at best could provide a salary of $3,500 a year.

What then is such a church to do? Close? Several members will ask, "What else can we do?" But others, displaying a wonderful stubbornness, will insist that their village must not be without an open church on Sundays. "We're going to keep this church open somehow!" "Somehow" often means that the church clerk calls my office at the Bangor Theological Seminary and asks for help. When a full-time minister cannot be found, then the Seminary is asked, "Can you supply us with a student pastor?"

For over 160 years the Seminary has furnished this service to scores of Maine churches. In fact the Seminary was founded in order to provide leaders for tiny congregations scattered through the country-side.

Back in 1810 Maine was considered by devout people to be a "vast, spiritually poverty-stricken territory." As a result a band of men and women met in 1814 to do something about the "one hundred and twenty thousand people in the district of Maine, who are mostly heathen." Out of their concern for the establishment and maintenance of village meeting houses the Seminary was born. At present were it not for the "school of the prophets" on the hill at least fifty congregations would be forced to bolt their doors to Sunday worship.

Each year these churches call upon the services of student pastors — some of whom are responsible to more than one small church. Almost all Maine counties include at least one student charge. Several denominations use the aid of student pastors: Baptist, Methodist, United Church of Christ (Congregational), Unitarian-Universalist. Although Presbyterian students enroll at this seminary, there is but a handful of Presbyterian Churches in Maine; thus students of this denomination are welcomed into the pulpits of other denominations while retaining their identity as Presbyterians.

Although Bangor Seminary has an enrollment of over one hundred, a number of students are unavailable as pastors. First year students are not eligible, nor are those who are failing in studies. Some students prefer to give all their attention to their books and courses; others, although committed to religious work, do not yet feel impelled to witness to their faith through preaching or pastoral work. Nearly one quarter of the students, for one reason or another, do not become student pastors.

The majority of students who serve churches are about thirty years of age although some are younger and several are much older. A few years ago a man of fifty-seven enrolled for theological study and brought forth the facetious remark from a far younger student, "You'll graduate just in time to retire, won't you?"

Many students, lacking college degrees, must take two years of college work in the pre-theological department of the Seminary before entering upon the three-year divinity course. After receiving the Seminary diploma for five years of successful study, two more years of liberal arts college work are required before they receive B.A. and Master of Divinity degrees, which will make them eligible for ordination.

Sometime after the first year of study students will begin to think seriously about assuming the responsibility of parish service, and soon they will be placed in a church. Their placement is arranged through the field education office of the Seminary and it is my task as director of this work to keep in touch with churches and students during their years of service. I seek to do this by visiting members of the churches where students are serving and inquiring about their effectiveness.

Since as many as fifty-two churches are served by students my "check-up" on the students' parish work is neither as frequent nor as thorough as it should be. Nonetheless my visits upon six to sixteen church members in a single parish usually reveal students' strengths and weaknesses.

After these visits I share my discoveries with the students, commending them when they are giving the best that can be expected of a student, and pointing out areas of their ministry that need added emphasis.

These beginning parsons are human; they know it and they hope the people in the churches they serve know it and accept the fact. Every student pastor rebels against the picture of a minister wearing a halo of a saintly character who is especially pious, especially righteous. They themselves know only too well that, whether in the pulpit or out, ministers are no symbols of righteousness. The student pastors whose names I call in the following pages make mistakes, get angry, cherish prejudices, seek preferment, fail to live up to commitments, sometimes let down the people they are called to serve. Yes they do. But nine out of every ten are working for God faithfully and churches productively in the time they have away from their studies. Conscious that they are imperfect and that all too often they deny the Lord and fail their congregations, still they give themselves with amazing devotion. Their lives are split three ways: church, studies, family (many have large families — it is a commonplace for a man with a wife and five children to enroll at Bangor). Seminarians have an almost impossible challenge to meet. That so many do meet it is the wonder of my life and the joy of my job.

The incidents from the diary that are set down here are authentic. The dates of the entries run from September (when the Seminary opens) through June of the following year. *The events recorded did not take place in any one school year but have been selected from several years; my thought being to choose those happenings that can best tell the story of small Down East congregations and the students who serve them.*

Walter L. Cook
Bangor, Maine
January 1978

September 22

This Monday morning my secretary brought my mail into the office saying she hoped it didn't contain any "grief," meaning she hoped the letters would not report any big fusses in the churches served by students. She got her good wish; there was no bad news. Apparently the congregations had enjoyed a quiet weekend, and I was relieved that no pastor had eloped with his church treasurer, or that no fretful student had hit an obnoxious sexton over the head with a candelabrum.

When a Bangor Seminary student begins work in a parish the people in the pews often make the following remark: "He's a student just starting out; we can't expect him to have all the common sense and leadership ability of an experienced pastor."

This expresses the generous attitude of almost all church members served by student pastors. These good people astonish and encourage me by their sympathy toward the unskilled labor of students.

Now and then, however, I hear from or visit some church member who is pleased by no student at all. No matter how energetic or able the student, this critic is rough on him; he seems to demand in a minister the combined talents of Billy Graham, Albert Schweitzer, Peter Marshall, and Norman Vincent Peale. But send such a synthetic personality to be his pastor and this discontented brother would still be sitting on the fault-finder's bench. What chance has a student with him? Representing settled opposition he mutters, complains, and laments, no matter whom I send.

Not all objectors *mutter*, however, some yell. For them, spotting a preacher's weaknesses seems exciting sport.

Far down in Washington County lives one of the most nimble kickers of all time. I never fail to run into him when visiting in his community; he never misses an opportunity to tell me everything. I met him the other day in the village Post Office and was pressed to step over to his house to hear the woeful story of the present pastor's baleful performance.

Panting to unload, my host offered me a seat on the top step of his porch, lighted a wet and mangled cigar stub, and let drive. His string of grievances was so long he invited me to lunch to hear him out. "The preacher is lazy, the preacher is an operator, the preacher is an egotist, the preacher is a liar." He is, at bottom, a skunk.

Rocked by the cannonade of criticism that continued from soup to hamburg to squash pie, I began to believe I'd need to advise the student to resign. Obviously this foe could never be won over. Getting the parson thrown out of church and town seemed to be a passion.

Later, when the host had finished another powerful cigar, I got up to leave. He followed me to the door still breathing slaughter. As I said goodbye he fished a five-dollar bill from his beat-up jeans. "Here," he growled, "give this to the preacher, he's having a pretty hard time."

September 23

Not all church members are eager or even willing

to "open up" when I visit them and ask for an evaluation of their student pastor's work. During the last few weeks I've encountered several who were reluctant to talk, who thought it would be a betrayal if they disclosed his weaknesses. When I protested that I am not an enemy spy, but the student's teacher and friend, interested, with all other faculty members, in his growth, much of their reluctance was banished.

Today student Richard Hetzel told me I need not go to *his* parish to discover from church members whether he needs more guidance and closer supervision. He knows already about all of his weaknesses: one of his members has just leveled with him completely. Hetzel confessed to me that for the last three months he has been receiving a kind of opposition to his work in the community. The church he serves is one of the most beautifully located of all churches served by students. A lovely lake, with a view of rugged hills and woods-crested mountains provides a setting so enchanting that many prefer to worship God "in nature," rather than attend inside services. Attendance at morning services has been falling off. Nobody has been openly critical of Dick, but he has felt sure that some church officials have been mumbling in their beards.

Last Tuesday he got it — all the criticism he could take packed into one evening! One of his deacons, Hetzel said, "got ginned up, rang the parsonage doorbell, came in where my wife and I and the kids were eating supper. He sat in a chair near the table and gave me a detailed report on everybody's opinion on what I'm doing that I'm not supposed to be doing, and what I'm not doing that I ought to be doing. So now, Dr. Cook, you know the technique: when you want the facts about your student pastors, get into dialogues with boozed-up deacons."

September 24

Student ministers, when conducting worship, vary bewilderingly in what they wear in the pulpits of the churches they serve. Some prefer a suit of quiet color, others choose a panoply: gown, clerical collar, tabs, stole, and even crosses and pins attached to the gowns. Some, liturgically minded, wear colored stoles appropriate to seasons of the church year.

(Students surely see variety in pulpit garb when faculty members conduct Seminary chapel services. During the same week one professor will wear an elaborate clerical dress, another a sport coat and a turtleneck jersey.)

On a recent Sunday at the Methodist church in East Corinth the student pastor bloomed in scarlet stole. The church sanctuary, though neither ugly nor barren, is quite plainly appointed so that the preacher's gorgeous apparel gave him a far higher profile than his surroundings required. The worshipers were dazzled — and puzzled — by all the colored splendor. Liking the young man, not wishing to hurt his feelings by registering their consternation to him, they asked me to tell him they would prefer less gaudy raiment in the pulpit.

So today I decided to talk over the matter with him and began by inquiring whether the flaming color of the stole he wore Sundays was ceremonially appropriate. "Oh," he said, "I don't wear it as a symbol of anything; it's just to cover up the moth holes in my gown."

September 26

Everybody arrived early for our chapel service here at the Seminary this morning. The leader was an import, a bigwig from Methodist headquarters; in fact, a bishop. After being introduced and apologizing for the bad weather he brought with him from Boston, he got our attention in a hurry by making several statements designed to start us off wide awake. He remarked jokingly that some people are so certain they can do all they plan to do that they write their diaries a week ahead!

If there is one job in the world where uncertainty is the only certainty it is mine. I would not dare to write my diary even one day ahead about how a student will succeed when he goes to work as pastor of his first church.

Outstanding students in classrooms sometimes do not live up to expectations as church workers. Other students who show little promise in studies seize opportunities to serve churches and become vigorous workers, thoughtful preachers, and helpful pastors.

This past summer I arranged for the placement of seven new student ministers in churches as far west as Upton and North Newry, as far east as Princeton, and as far north as Oakfield. Predicting how they would get along in their parishes was impossible.

Strangely, some student who relates well to his fellow students will quickly be at loggerheads with church people. The "A" student in the classroom may be a "D-minus" pastor in a church. A timid, shrinking personality on campus may become a prophet of boldness in the pulpit. A cold and reserved person here may become warm and responsive there. The fellow who is teachable in all his academic work may be opinionated and altogether fatheaded when meeting with his congregation's official board. Hypersensitive to critical remarks in the Seminary social room, a student may be as thick-shelled as a mud turtle to the sarcasms of the music committee chairperson of a church.

I just never can tell what will happen when these raw recruits hit their first parish.

The Seminary's ironclad rule that no new student shall serve as a pastor until he has been at the school two full semesters is at least a limited safeguard against churches getting hurt by undesirable student leadership. During two semesters after he arrives we come to know a little about him — that he pays his bills, doesn't plagiarize term papers, is industrious and intelligent enough to pass courses.

But the little we learn about him at school is too little to estimate exactly how well or badly he will acquit himself in a parish. The unexpected is always happening with student pastors.

Here was a student who had always lived in a large city. I would have expected him to relate clumsily to a small countryside church in northern Maine. Surely he would feel ill at ease, miscast, unable to relate and to communicate. This simply was not true of Edwin Hoysradt. He came to Seminary from New

York City where he had lived all his life — forty-five years. He had been a bankteller; was always well-dressed and polished, urbane without being suave, a sure candidate for a suburban church. How could a New York City background prepare Ed for mixing with people involved with Aroostook potatoes, deer hunting, pulp cutting, and trout fishing?

Just fine. He served in "The County" two years as a student and remained several years after graduation as a full-time minister.

September 29

One of our young juniors drove to Carmel yesterday to preach his first sermon in the Union Church; after the service he dropped by to tell me how it went. I gather he was really scared as he paced back and forth on the road in front of the church, then in the vestibule, waiting to face a congregation of about fifty worshipers. He must have looked so jittery and jumpy that a kindly deacon inquired, "Are you going to be sick, do you think?"

"No," replied the lad, "I'm not sick; I'm just petrified. I'm frightened out of my mind. Some of the people in the church were Christians before I was born. I'm sure when it comes time for me to pray and preach I'll collapse."

"Young man," said the deacon, "it might help if you'll remember one thing: the congregation isn't expecting very much."

In our conversation this morning I asked the boy whether he was requested by the church to return to conduct another service. "Did your listeners have a word of appreciation for you after you prayed and preached without collapsing?"

"Why yes," he admitted, with a slightly bewildered look in his eye, "they did at that. They even asked me to preach next Sunday. But one lady, very blunt, said she was surprised how anybody as young as I could say anything in a sermon that an adult would find interesting or profitable. She ordered me to 'stick with the Bible' when I preach there again so I won't be guilty of a lot of foolish talk."

Of course I fully expect a young fellow of twenty-two to be scared on Sunday morning as he drives slowly along the road and hesitatingly parks his car in front of the church where he will preach his first sermon and pray his first public prayer, but I was surprised to find another seminarian, forty-seven years old, who was also close to panic.

This latter fellow, suffering from an attack of pulpit phobia, was a fighter pilot in World War II, a survivor of many missions over Europe. Face to face with his first preaching mission, half inclined to back out, he was so shaky and fidgety that he came to my office for encouragement. I tried my best to put heart into him but he remained fearful that he'd keel over when he was in front of the congregation. I mentioned to him that he must have been in even greater danger in the Air Force. "Oh," he groaned, "flying was nothing compared to preaching this sermon."

September 30

My passion for fly-casting on northern Maine ponds is pretty well known on the Seminary campus.

All kinds of remarks, to which I must confess I leave myself wide open, come from students who know my relish for the sport.

This morning after chapel I posted a notice on the bulletin board: CLASS IN HOMILETICS CAN-CELED TOMORROW (WEDNESDAY).

After the notice had been up an hour or two I was greeted by all kinds of whimsical observations as I appeared here and there about the campus:

"So, class canceled tomorrow. How about that! Suppose you'll be up in Baxter Park on some of the trout ponds you're always talking about. And here we are slaving at our studies."

"Take me along, will yer? Me and the wife and our starving kids can use a trout dinner."

"If it rains hard tomorrow and you can't go fish-ing, I suppose you'll have class after all." (This last comment was wide of the mark; a dedicated sportsman will fish for hours in a belting rain and love every minute of it.)

No malice in the students' quips, just good fun. But how could they know? I'm going to sit in a den-tist's chair for an hour, not in a canoe on a trout pond.

The last roguish remark about my hobby was late in the afternoon; this one had to do with my fishing tackle. It came from a student pastor whose church is in Ellsworth. "Hey, Mr. Cook, how about borrowing your landing net?" The request surprised me, I didn't know he was a fisherman. It turned out he's not, but had another use for the net. "If you'll lend me that thing to take up Sunday morning offerings in my church we'll soon have our new electric organ paid

9

for by increased contributions." I couldn't figure that one out so he explained: "The net's an ideal offering plate. Coins would fall through and make a racket on the pews and on our hardwood floor, and cause red faces; only the bills would stay netted."

October 2

Many Maine churches are served by students who have enrolled at the Seminary at great risk. They have sold their homes, uprooted their families, and given up good paying jobs because they believe God wants them to be ministers.

Today William Baran became the student pastor at the Norridgewock Federated Church. How will he get along? I have high hopes for him as he goes out. Will the spirit of this tall, pleasant-faced man be bolstered as he encounters the demands a parish puts upon a student minister or will his hopes be blighted?

Baran burned all his bridges before coming to the Seminary. He struggled through his first-year courses: history, philosophy, Greek, English, psychology, English Bible. Now he has gone out to serve a church as a beginning pastor. His experiences in his first parish will color his whole view of the ministry.

Bill is full of hope and glad expectancy, but he is also apprehensive. He says quite seriously, *"I'm* praying that the work will go well, and I'll be getting the prayers of much better people than I am, to help me."

October 5

The mixed motives of students are often evident

when they come to my office and say, "I've been thinking about it, and I've decided I'd like a chance to serve
a church." Besides a desire to serve God and work
with people in a parish, they are probably thinking
about a salary — however small — that will help them
pay a few Seminary bills.

It is extremely hard on some men, especially those
over thirty, who have previously been successful in
other professions or in business, to surrender the
breadwinning role in the family. It's a blow to a husband's pride to be dependent upon his wife while he
attends lectures, writes term papers, and takes exams.

Recently, just before a Seminary faculty meeting,
Professor Szikszai remarked about a certain student,
"No wonder he's one of our outstanding men, he
has brains, dedication, industry, strong convictions —
and a wife who's working his way through school."

October 8

Chuck Schleich is the student minister in Albany,
a village in Oxford County. It must be close to 160
miles from the Seminary. These young fellows think
nothing of weekend drives to their distant parishes
that would be killers to older men and women.

Two Sundays ago he arrived at the quaint little
church once served by the Reverend Hilda Ives, who
became known as an eloquent preacher in scores of
Maine's town and country churches.

As Chuck pushed open the door of the church at
service time he glanced back at the parking lot:
not a single car in it; and none parked along the roadside. He found the church empty: no organist, no

11

sexton, and no worshipers — a most demoralizing situation for a preacher who had driven from Bangor almost into New Hampshire, and had painstakingly prepared a sermon.

Schleich sat in the big chair behind the pulpit and waited: five minutes, ten minutes, fifteen. No one showed for the meeting.

Although the congregation seldom fills the church, a few are always present. Finally the crestfallen parson walked down the aisle, out the door, and began an investigation. At last he found the entire congregation in an apple orchard — not engaged in worship.

The following Sunday with the owner's permission he conducted a service in the orchard at eight a.m. Twenty-five were present. A Bible, a cross, and offering plates on stacked apple boxes comprised the worship center. A view of the New Hampshire White Mountains and trees heavy with Northern Spies did not detract at all from an atmosphere of devotion. The service was made up of prayers, the singing of mimeographed hymns, scripture readings, and an offering.

The congregation didn't come to church; so Schleich took the church to the congregation. Next year, come apple-picking time, he'll know where to look for his Sunday-morning worshipers.

October 9

One of the more remote student parishes is a Methodist church in Patten, 135 miles from the Seminary. Henry Huddleston — tall, ruddy-cheeked, round-bellied, and most genial — is the pastor. Right now Henry is dissatisfied with his preaching. His sermons, he thinks, are not lively enough to keep the congregation wide awake. He said today: "A doctor friend told me that when the eyes are closed the hearing becomes more acute. I told him that I'd noticed a lot of people experimenting with that theory when I was about three-quarters of the way through my Sunday sermons."

Many good-humored remarks are passed around by student ministers about church members who fall asleep during Sunday morning worship. The latest variation on this habit was reported by Raymond Blaisdell, pastor of the church in Brooks. Last Sunday, an early fall day, was unusually warm. The thermometer outside the hardware store in the village registered 82 degrees F. Inside the church auditorium, drowsiness prevailed in half the pews as the over-heated congregation languidly sang, "Stand Up, Stand Up For Jesus," while remaining seated.

One of the ushers, after he had finished guiding worshipers to their pews, sat down in a chair at the rear of the sanctuary and just plain fell asleep. Blaisdell, conducting worship, announced the morning prayer. The usher, who had been all but snoring, unaccountably awoke during silent prayer, looked about, concluded that the minister had just announced the offering, jumped to his feet and began passing the collection plate. He got started in this operation just when student Blaisdell with closed eyes began the pastoral prayer. Offering taking and prayer continued simultaneously. The congregation stopped praying and started reaching — a worship pattern both amusing and confusing.

Blaisdell's later comment was, "Probably such a procedure will not be generally adopted by churches alert to changing designs in worship patterns."

Drowsiness was also the cause of embarrassment in a Dexter church a few Sundays ago. Because the regular minister of the church was ill, I was asked to send a student substitute to conduct worship. As the student began the sermon the organist slipped out the rear door of the choir loft and descended to the vestry for a smoke. She felt she could relax a bit, and sinking into an easy chair fell asleep. The student delivered a brief sermon, announced the closing hymn — and waited. Everybody was ill-at-ease: choir, congregation, especially the preacher. After a painful silence, the student (possessing no singing voice of distinction) started the first stanza of the closing hymn without the help of the organ.

Strains of the hymn filtered down to the sleeping organist, who awoke with a start and appeared at the back door of the choir loft with a very red face. Title of the hymn: "Awake, My Soul, Stretch Every Nerve."

October 12

Today I conducted worship for a really solemn-faced congregation in the Dover-Foxcroft Baptist Church. This fellowship has a resident member-ship of about 170 and is probably the liveliest religious group in a town of 4200. They can't seem to lure a shepherd from any part of Maine to tend the flock.

Were they glum! After the service I sat down with the pulpit committee in the vestry and tried to coax a few smiles from them with a couple attempts at drollery and a pun or two. I guess they felt inwardly that I had a dislocated sense of humor. They continued glum.

And they do have a reason. The committee has, with unsuccessful result, explored all the usual sources of ministerial supply. Discouraged in their efforts to find a full-time parson they have turned to the Seminary for help, asking whether I can provide a student minister.

I rehearsed for them the limitations of student ministers: not ordained, must spend at least four and a half days a week at school, lack years of experience.

Still the committee insisted it would like to hear a Seminary student as a candidate. The only other possible applicant for the pulpit is a retired minister living in Massachusetts. So the question was: shall the Dover church seek the services of a young inexperienced minister or of an elderly retired minister? "Well," declared one committee member, "let's try the young fellow; better our church should be a training ground than a dumping ground."

October 14

"I spend hours trying to prepare helpful sermons. I preach them to people who seem to be listening, but

15

nothing happens afterwards. Nothing gets done, not a soul reforms, nobody gets mad even."

This is from a discouraged student pastor. The same pessimism is often reflected in many conversations I have held with seasoned, full-time ministers.

But good sermons do bring results. I think back over my interviews with many members of churches served by students. During the last twenty-two years many lay people have told me of helpful, even searching sermons they have heard delivered by beginning preachers.

A student preaching on Mount Desert Island — and an alcoholic is so encouraged that he seeks out the pastor for further talks and is now sober.

A student preaching in Pittsfield — and a couple whose marriage is all but on the rocks is inspired to stay together and really try again.

A student preaching in Winslow — and a teenage thief, conscience awakened, returns a stolen sweater to its owner and takes the consequences.

A student preaching in Ellsworth — and a discouraged young public school teacher ready to resign is spurred to stay with her work. She says, "That sermon of his put heart into me."

A student preaching in Damariscotta — and a capable but apathetic church member is roused to get into town affairs, runs for selectman, and becomes a force for righteousness.

Now and then, students preach forceful sermons with reverse English on them. Just this morning I heard of a telling example. Edward Higgins, student minister of the Howland Methodist Church, preached a sermon last August that got results, tangible ones.

In the sermon he used an illustration that contained information about kinds of fish that become wormy in late summer. The lay leader of the Howland church is the owner of a fish market. Two weeks after Higgins used his fish illustration the merchant told him: "That fish story of yours damaged my business. Fish sales in my market are down by half. Please," urged the proprietor, "no more stories in sermons about wormy fish."

October 19

The air was crisp this morning, and it seemed, as I drove along the highway from Bangor to New Sharon, that every maple was on fire. I drove into the village, crossed Sandy River, turned right, and there was the church where I was to attend worship. I slipped into a back pew just as the organist was concluding her prelude: "Panis Angelicus." (I always sit far back so that the student will not become distracted by my note-taking during the sermon.) As I settled back I got a real start; I couldn't believe it. I was staring at a hand-pumped pipe organ. My soul! I thought they'd gone out with the last century.

I must confess I was as much interested in that old thing as I was in the sensible sermon delivered by the student.

The organ stood in the front left-hand corner of the meeting house, the pump handle extending toward the pulpit. An improvised green cloth screen partially concealed the pumper: a strapping fifteen-year-old boy, who, during the sermon, came out of hiding and sat in a front pew. The manually inflated music producer brought memories of the little Baptist Church in East Rochester, New Hampshire, where my father was minister fifty years ago. The pumping process as I observed it today was at least silent, though partly visible. The operation I remember so long ago created, through squeaks and thumps, as much sound as came from the faded gilt pipes themselves.

After the service in New Sharon was over I snooped behind the organ, with the organist's permission, for a closer view of the pumping apparatus. Besides a box with a foam rubber seat for the pumper were the following: a stack of gospel song books, a spilled-over heap of antiquated church school "quarterlies," a cracked vase containing five dusty wax red roses, a huge pulpit Bible looking as though it had been pounded by scores of ministerial fists, and a neatly piled cache of comic magazines.

Although surprised to see a hand-pumped organ still in use I do know as many as fifty Maine churches where the old foot-pedal organs are stashed away in corners. Most village congregations now have an electric organ replacing the old square museum piece. Not knowing what to do with an obsolete instrument, and lacking courage or authority to sell or destroy it, the church janitor (with the help of a trustee) has shoved it into one end of the balcony, or toted it to the basement to stand beside the oil heater, or left it in the vestibule partly covered with a faded cloth. It sits there, one fancy-carpeted foot-pedal askew, two keys stuck down, the diapason stop missing. It gathers dust, awaiting the day when it will become old and dilapidated enough to be sold as an antique.

The East Eddington Church, out on the Airline a dozen miles from the Joshua Chamberlain Bridge, makes use of a venerable organ that once was hand pumped, but is now equipped with an electric blower. The organ contains several wooden pipes one of which, Gertrude McGinley tells me (she has sung in the choir for forty-five years), has to be removed each year and shaken vigorously to dislodge a persistent wood mouse. The mouse must so much love the old hymns of the church that it persistently rebuilds its nest in the pipe.

October 21

Old organs are being discarded but not old hymns — or "gospel songs" as they are more properly called.

Tonight I attended a meeting in the Canaan Community Church where a new electric organ was dedicated. After a lengthy recital on the instrument by a visiting organist of modest talent, the student minister invited the audience to call for numbers of special songs they would like to sing together. Three old favorites were requested, which the congregation sang with enthusiasm: "The Old, Rugged Cross," "In the Garden," and "Nearer My God To Thee."

At no place is a Bangor Seminary professor farther removed from the average worshiper in the student parish than in hymnody. Again and again in Seminary classes, student ministers are encouraged to guide church members to appreciate and sing "great" hymns, free of sentimentality and fuzzy theology.

The students listen and set out to reform the taste of people they serve by proposing more thoughtful and elevating hymns. To little avail. The people in the pews just go right on loving, and wanting to sing, the songs they consider special, which many sophisticated clergymen and divinity professors label trifling and shallow.

Repeatedly church members complain to me, "Why does our minister insist on singing hymns that we've never sung before and can't sing when we try?" So, I often encourage student ministers to hold Sunday evening hymn-sings when they can introduce the more stately hymns of the church, a few at a time. Several have tried this scheme. But, even after several hymn-sings, when the members of a congregation are invited to call out the numbers of hymns, inevitably they ask for, and sing with enthusiasm, "The Old, Rugged Cross," "In the Garden," and "Nearer My God To Thee"!

October 22

When I pushed open the door to my office this morning I saw four letters on my desk. One was from the clerk of the Federated Church in Temple. I opened that one last. I anticipated bad news and was not disappointed. The good folks in this far away hamlet are much dissatisfied with their present student minister. Will I please be prepared to receive him back at the Seminary. (My foreknowledge of the bad news does not make me a clairvoyant. Three or four weeks ago this student had stated, "I can't do anything out there. That town is the world capital

20

of desolation." I was much concerned about his assessment, but had decided to wait and see. Quite clearly, the waiting was over, and the seeing was at hand.)

The clerk wrote: "We don't really expect much of a student out here, just decent sermons, and if somebody dies we want him to conduct the burial service. We haven't anything bad to say about this student's character; the whole trouble with him is his attitude."

During the afternoon I drove out to Temple to inquire about his "attitude." I learned that he is thought unfriendly, defeatist, negative, and, in particular, openly critical of the church building, the village, and the people of the congregation. Members I visited assured me that all who attend church can stand preaching that is "good and straight." They said, "We *want* a pastor to acquaint us with our need for reform, and to encourage us to do something about our need. But this lad of yours just grumbles all over the place and fusses that Temple people are a collection of hicks. Never one word of encouragement comes from him. He even goes into Farmington and blats that we are backward and stubborn."

The village of Temple is about six miles west of Farmington. Admittedly, the vistas of the community are limited (except for an enchanting prospect of Mount Blue). Highway 43 into Temple from Farmington is the only road, and a short distance beyond the town, the road ends. The church building is small and has but one room to house a Sunday school of thirty to forty children each weekend. The worshiping congregation is usually made up of no more than a dozen of the faithful — most of them elderly. All this, however, should be challenging.

How different this student is from the one who served the Temple church a few years ago. That young man moved in, sized up the potential, and worked where he could: preaching compassionate sermons (and nudging sermons, too) to an often dispirited people. Faithfully he visited not only the sick and shut-ins, but all families who were even remotely related to the church, giving himself warmly and generously to all who needed him.

Only a few students are at loggerheads with congregations they serve. Disputes between pastors and church members do arise, but most members of student-led charges are patient; and usually students are teachable and humble enough to realize that the churches they serve have been around a long while and must be guided by patient concern if changes and reforms are to begin.

October 26

Schoodic Lake in Piscataquis County can be mighty cold the last of October. I ought to know; I was in it this afternoon. At about two o'clock I baptized student Robert Boutwell near the south shore.

Bob had not been content with the form of baptism (sprinkling) he received as a small boy; so he asked me to immerse him — not in a comfortable baptistry in a well-heated church building, but in Schoodic, because it is near Brownville, where he is a student minister.

Bob's fellow students and at least two faculty mem-

22

bers could not convince him that an indoor baptism is unquestionably valid. "It's got to be in Schoodic Lake," he said.

So with pretty good grace, if not with finesse, I immersed him. The lake shore bottom was uncertain for wading, submerged rocks were slippery, and the wind blew. The occupants of a passing motor launch were understandably curious — and resorted to binoculars to study the remarkable tableau.

Bob was not embarrassed at all.

The shoreline congregation was comprised of the student's wife sitting on a log, holding a blanket-wrapped three-month-old baby; and an older son of two-and-a-half sitting on a big chocolate shaped rock singing lustily during the ceremony.

Honoring students' changing convictions is some-times inconvenient. I surely vote for summer im-mersions.

October 30

Last week a Congregational church in York County of about 85 members held its annual meeting and election of officers. The student pastor reported to me that although many important posts changed hands, there was one office that is filled every year by the same man: the office of Chronic Kicker.

His election is always uncontested; he has no run-ner-up even.

The student came into my office and indulged him-self in a talking jag. Over a coffee cup he gave me the details about this constant complainer, who is a fault-finder, dejection-dispenser, and settled opponent of anything that looks like progress.

To my surprise the student said the guy's muttering and growling is sometimes downright helpful.

It seems that a church school teacher mentioned the sad state of the church school classrooms to some members of the congregation who had lingered near the rear of the sanctuary after the close of a Sunday morning's worship. She expressed the wish that the church would provide funds to enlarge the cramped quarters available to teachers and pupils.

The listening church members murmured understandingly. But plainly they were more apathetic than sympathetic and started to think about Sunday dinner and an afternoon of leisurely TV. They began to drift toward the door.

Just at this moment the kicker approached from the front of the church, and hearing the teacher's request, immediately and loudly opposed the prospect of any building improvement: "The whole idea is ridiculous, enough room is available right now if properly distributed, any such project would cost too much, and anyhow this is a maneuver on the part of the Sunday school superintendent to put something over on the congregation."

That did it. The outburst galvanized the church members present, who put Sunday dinner out of their minds for a few minutes. All at once they got a vision of several well-furnished classrooms where conditions would be vastly improved for youngsters' study. "Let's call a meeting of the congregation," they said, "and get this thing going."

"So," said the grinning student, looking into his empty coffee cup, "I'll never again knock a kicker. He can sure be useful."

October 31

"The members of the church I serve are the finest people in the world, but one thing about them bothers me: I do wish they weren't so shy about expressing their faith!"

This morning a Seminary student, more enthusiastically religious than some, lamented to me that the folk in his congregation are reluctant to witness to their faith in God. "They're selling short their God and their neighbors because they are tongue-tied about the most important thing in the world. They'll talk about everything but their religion."

(My own guess is that the average church member would be less embarrassed to be caught with a book about sex tucked under his arm than he would be if he were caught carrying a Bible.)

November 1

A report reached my office this morning that a church near Skowhegan has picked up a floater for its parson. This is much the same as picking up the bug during a flu epidemic.

A floater is a disaster.

He has a profile that is unmistakable to the wary: he is a smooth, religious-talking guy who hovers around a town where he's heard the people in a certain church are dissatisfied with the present minister. The floater may or may not be ordained, but he calls himself a preacher. He's been wistfully eyeing the church's cozy parsonage for weeks, waiting for the present occupant to move out so he can get a chance to move in.

He has already tried out the ministry in other towns in other states (as well as in Maine) and bombed his opportunities every time. He has no credentials, is cutting pulp at the moment, or raking blueberries, or serving as deputy sheriff, or driving a school bus. Not content with these most honorable ways of earning a living, he's been impatiently waiting to exploit some unsuspecting church by providing his services.

When the present parson vacates the parish the floater makes his pitch.

To be sure, he has characteristics and qualities that appeal to boards of deacons and trustees. He'll offer to serve the church for just free-will collections, exhibits an affable personality, sings well, conducts services informally, is supplied with an unlimited inventory of twice-told anecdotes, and is a facile speaker.

Because he acknowledges no denominational ties he'll invite the church fathers to renege on any commitment the congregation may have made to support a state or national benevolence fund. (This is sure to be alluring to several economy-minded and influential members of the trustee board.)

He gets the call to the church which believes it has a real bargain. The members say: "This parson preaches from the Bible and he isn't long-winded. When he gets through pumping he lets go the handle."

But after performing with a flair for a few months the chinks in his character begin to show. Bits and pieces of information begin to drift into town that he left some sticky problems in the last community where he held forth. Then too the word begins to get around that in his present charge all is not well. The local garageman, the fuel oil dealer, the hardware store manager slowly awake to the knowledge that the "Reverend seems to think he's exempt from paying his bills." Other dubious revelations from the past and in the present follow. Dawning on the minds of an increasing number of church members is the suspicion that they have no bargain for a pastor but a phony.

After about a year the deacons and trustees who ushered in the floater with jubilation want to ride him out of town on a rail.

Inwardly they mumble, "We've been had."

November 3

This morning I hadn't got the key into my office door before a student, who serves a church near South Paris, descended on me, trouble written all over his face. After getting in and switching on the light, I sat down. *He* wouldn't — or couldn't. He looked haunted. Right away he blurted: "Got a wedding coming."

Well, I knew it wasn't *his;* already he has a wife and two children. Probably his own wedding caused him less panic than the one he now had on his mind, one over which he must preside as the "officiating clergyman."

"It's a church wedding, too," he groaned, "a real big deal: four ushers, four bridesmaids, flower girl, ring bearer, soloist, and after the ceremony a receiving line! What's a man to do?"

First I handed him a chart showing where a wedding party stands at the front of a church while the service is conducted, then I recommended to him a service manual containing sample marriage ceremonies, and finally offered him a cup of coffee over which he could more thoroughly air his misgivings.

(The church he serves has several overfastidious members who want every little thing in place. They can be uncommonly finicky about details. Any boggle by the preacher and they'd be vexed. I did not reveal this to the nervous young parson.)

The student reported that besides his own wedding, which took place six years before, he had attended but one other. Said he: "Didn't even know what was going on at the first, didn't pay much attention to the second. But brother, if I'd known then I was going to become a parson and marry couples myself, I wouldn't have missed a move."

Later, next semester, in my field education class he will participate in a mock wedding which will provide at least some guidance for him. Unfortunately the couple who want to be married in three weeks are unwilling to wait until the pastor furthers his education! At the moment he would gladly have traded all he'd learned in the Seminary about the authorship of Ephesians for a thorough knowledge of marriage service procedure.

The face of the student showed even deeper anxiety as he held out a sample copy of a legal document titled **CERTIFICATE OF MARRIAGE** obtained from

Jay Alley, Bangor's City Clerk, which must be filled out and returned to the Clerk's office after the ceremony. The student pointed to ominous words on the certificate: THE LAWS OF MAINE PROVIDE FOR A FINE NOT EXCEEDING ONE THOUSAND DOLLARS OR IMPRISONMENT NOT EXCEEDING FIVE YEARS TO BE THE PUNISHMENT OF ANY CLERGYMAN WHO SHALL SOLEMNIZE A MARRIAGE WITHIN THIS STATE UNLESS AUTHORIZED TO SOLEMNIZE MARRIAGE THEREIN.

"Suppose I do something wrong," he wailed, "instead of behind a pulpit I'll wind up behind bars."

I tried to comfort him; told him I've not known a single student minister to spend even one night in jail for violation of Maine laws for solemnizing weddings. I reminded him that this was not a funeral but a wedding he was to preside over, and that most weddings are happy, not melancholy affairs, also that he should cast gloom aside and get into the spirit of the thing.

(How was he to know, as he stood there in deep distress, that three weeks later he would swing into my office with a wedding carnation in his buttonhole and a broad grin on his face, to report to me that after all his fretting he had tied the knot without suffering a nervous breakdown?)

November 4

Seldom do I read carefully the bulletin board in the Seminary mail room; I'd need a solid half-hour to find my way through the thick cloud of notices. Today, smack in the middle of the board, appeared a large sign: SEX — in big flaring letters. What now, I wondered, and moved nearer to investigate! Beneath the three huge letters was a bit of advertising that read, "Now that we have your attention, please accept our invitation to attend the Bond Lecture in the Chapel Building at 7:30 tonight to hear Dorothy Clarke Wilson, noted Maine author and lecturer."

(Maybe some student pastor will conclude that such alluring advertisements will go over big on the bulletin board in the vestibule of the church he serves. If he tries something like it, I'll surely be getting a call from one of his trustees.)

November 6

The members of the Ellsworth Congregational Church can boast of having one of the most attractive religious structures in Maine. It doesn't sprawl and spread, but stands compact and sedate on a hillside near the town's center, painted white with a high graceful steeple. Right now the pastor is a student, but surely this will not prevail. The congregation is certain to enlarge its vision, stretch its treasury, and call a full-time minister. The student who serves the church is a bit on the gusty side and outwardly sure of himself; intelligent, but oh so sure of himself.

On my drive down from Bangor I speculated on the report I would get from one of the deacons who is an official of Union Trust, a leading and venerable local bank. For forty years he's been watching parsons come and go. When I asked him how the church

30

people were responding to their new minister I got a guarded answer. The deacon was not about to commit himself until he knew the young man for a much longer time.

The deacon's lack of hurry to reach a conclusion is typical of lay officials in many Maine churches, and provides seasoning experience for student pastors who expect almost upon arrival to find instant and enthusiastic acceptance.

If a young preacher anticipates acclaim for a sermon he thinks is unusually helpful, he may go home to Sunday dinner crestfallen to tell his wife: "Guess that sermon of mine was no masterpiece after all. Nobody had a word of praise for it." Even if the pastor has bright ideas that triple Sunday service attendance and double the heft of the collection plates at offering time, he should not expect that all he needs to do from then on is to listen to everybody's spoken admiration.

Some students who come here from outside New England expect more vocal recognition than they get when they turn in impressive preaching and pastoral performances. Not receiving rapturous praise and delirious approval for brilliant sermons or conspicuous administrative talent in their church work, these students often label Mainers standoffish, aloof, tight-lipped, and even unfriendly.

For myself I find it hard to imagine an effusive lobsterman, a demonstrative poultryman, a cutter of pulp ready to burst forth, a blueberry raker pouring out compliments. State of Maine people do appreciate good work well done, but many live up to their reputation for reserve.

November 8

All about Bushey's bushy beard.

One of our Seminary juniors, Richard Bushey, is serving the Franklin United Methodist Church. Dick is a discerning student, much alive to all public issues which involve social justice. About a month ago he decided to grow a beard, and the result of his decision came on very black and very heavy.

A cry of anguish went up from members of the congregation: "You look like a hippy. Shave it please, we come to church to worship God, not to be reminded of hippies."

Bushey, feeling that such a demand was an invasion of his privacy, an attempt to trample his freedom, refused to cut off the offending foliage. The battle was joined. The parishioners slapped down an ultimatum: "Shave the beard or resign the church."

The young fellow tendered his resignation, but members of the congregation did some second thinking and concluded they'd been making a fuss over not much. They notified Bushey that they did not accept his resignation and requested him to conduct worship the following Sunday — beard and all.

Much small mindedness abounds on both sides these days over hair and whiskers. Seminary students claim some churches are petty in their objections to long hair and beards; I have to point out to students that they themselves are petty when they insist on having their own way on such a picayune matter.

(A fourteen-year-old boy in a Sebago Lake area church school class, defending his long-haired young minister, felt he'd clinched the matter: "Jesus had long hair didn't he? All the pictures I've ever seen of him showed him that way.")

November 9

So often it happens at Bangor Seminary: some students dull in Greek, Hebrew, theology, philosophy, and Bible interpretation are able to shine brightly in church work. The results of tests show that many such students could excel in the classroom as well as in the parish.

The student minister of the Carmel Union Church has a lively interest in feeding his people as a good shepherd but has little interest in feeding his own mind as an earnest student. When I reported at our Thursday afternoon faculty meeting that the people in Carmel were enthusiastic about his efforts in the parish, a united groan went up from my colleagues: "He's putting in all his time at the church." Often students do give "too much church work" as an excuse for shoddy academic performance.

Sometimes the reasons given by students for below passing grades show much originality. Today, I heard a new excuse — passed on to me by the Seminary's Old Testament professor. The professor, dissatisfied with a student's classroom performance, accosted the man in the Canteen and Mail Room and pressed for a reason.

The encounter occurred on a recent Saturday while the student and the professor were the only ones in the room. The student glibly presented four pretexts for his academic deficiency, the last of which was a bit unusual: "I freeze when I have to take an exam; I don't find the course material helps me to write sermons; the class comes too early in the morning; I was stung by a tzetze fly."

At this point the dialogue was interrupted by the arrival of the Canteen attendant which left the professor to meditate upon a most beguiling explanation for the failure to pass Old Testament examinations.

November 12

For the last few weeks I have been sending student preachers deep into Washington County to supply pulpits at the Pembroke (Iron Works) and West Pembroke United Methodist Churches.

On Mondays, when I make the assignment to the Pembrokes (one student handles both churches), I give the student explicit instruction on how to choose the hymns for his services. The organs in both churches are in woeful straits. On one organ the "b" note refuses to sound; on the other the "f" is silent. Although the student preacher uses the same sermon and scripture lesson at both services, he must select different hymns in each worship hour to avoid those crippled notes. So, I advise the student to arrive at each church well before the time of service in order that he may thumb through the hymnbooks in search of worship songs that contain appropriately no "b" or "f."

This briefing is mostly for the student who might become so apprehensive over the uncertainty of the organ that sermon time would find him less than poised. It is also for the congregations and organists who would feel embarrassed by their churches' faulty equipment.

The chairman of the music committee at the Iron Works church commented to me when he described the organ's shortcomings, "If we do have to listen to any sour notes during our service, we prefer that they come from the preacher at sermon time, not from the organ at hymn time."

November 17

Jim Sleeper, a Seminary senior, has become the pastor of a coastal church where the congregation is a bit staid and sedate. Sleeper, who is free-wheeling, easy-going, and breezy, is also at times most inventive. No sooner had he arrived at the Freeport church then the local mortician called and asked him to conduct a funeral service for a man Jim did not know and had never even seen. Jim was in a dilemma: how could he "say a few kind words" about a person he had never met?

Finally, after much thought, mixed with some anxiety, he hit upon a scheme that would bring honor to the memory of the man. Hearing that the deceased had been an accomplished fiddler Jim secured a tape recording, made several months before, of the man playing his violin. Jim played it at the funeral service. "Turkey in the Straw" was the title of the selection.

The people attending the service were satisfied with the musical number as a substitute for a eulogy.

Funerals are often backgrounds for a grim wryness, as is illustrated by a recent service conducted in a parish not far from Ellsworth. The fine young parson, quiet spoken and reserved, presided over an unusual memorial service that taxed his theological sensibilities. Relatives of the deceased parishioner requested that his ashes be placed in two locations: one half in an urn, the other half scattered on the waves at a particular place on the Maine coast. The parson with what dignity he could muster complied.

The day after the event he dryly reported in my field education class that he had conducted a half-ashed funeral service.

November 18   9:30 a. m.

The Seminary Canteen and Mail Room on the ground floor of Maine Hall is often a center where lively discussions, theological and otherwise, occur. The room is small, and the much-used bulletin board, individual mail boxes, and coffee machine make for a milling mob, especially between classes.

This morning a loud exchange took place in front of the bulletin board about a picture in the *Bangor Daily News* that had been cut out and pinned to the board. The clipping showed a prominent Bangor pastor's shapely wife, in tights, toning up her physique in the Slimnastics class at the city "Y."

Half of the students labeled the publicizing of such body improvement activity undignified for a minister's wife. The other half were keen in defense of her right and "duty" to advertise her assent to physical fitness.

I reflected that the social standards for ministers' wives have changed in the last thirty-five years. The dignified matron image is fading, the "good Joe" is replacing it.

November 18   3:30 p. m.

A small contingent of student ministers' wives waited on me in my office. Perhaps the morning's heated talk in the Canteen about the lady in tights provoked their visit. At any rate they were inquiring about "our place" in communities where their husbands are serving churches. I commented on the wide divergence of standards for preachers' wives; then when pressed by the group to suggest dependable guidelines for correct conduct I fell back on a cliche: "Rely on your own good taste."

(A number of years ago in the North Anson parish a student's pretty wife attended an outdoor Sunday afternoon service in shorts. The deacons' wives were horrified, but the deacons were undismayed.)

November 22

On Hammond Street in Bangor stands the First Christian Church. To me the church seems a kind of rarity — inside at least. When strangers step through the door they get the feeling at first that they have entered a theater and not a church, because they are soon sitting in individual connecting seats rather than pews.

For the last thirty years the fellowship has been served mostly by students, all kinds of students — like the one who is there now: Robert Sansoucie.

Bob and I met on the campus this morning, and I could see he wanted to talk. So I put one foot on the huge stump of one of our recently cut elm trees and prepared to listen. He was hurting, and I soon saw why.

"It's this way," Bob said, "for about four months a certain lady attended Sunday services at First Christian, and I was thinking about asking her to unite with the church. All at once she dropped out of sight."

Bob explained to me that for a while he wondered whether he had accidentally stomped on her corns in one of his sermons. Then, just the day before Bob and I held our campus conversation, he met her on Harlow Street in front of the public library.

Fearless Bob. He plunged right in with his head down and demanded to know why she had stopped worshiping at First Christian. He got a crisp reply: "Young man," she said, "you've got a lot to learn about preaching sermons; when you've got it learned I'll come back and listen to you."

I took my foot off the stump and went sadly on my way. Part of my job at Bangor Seminary is to teach preaching.

November 24

I much admire the inventiveness of some student ministers as they conduct worship in small countryside churches where no choir is available in the service.

Yesterday, I visited a small student church in North Brooksville. No choir of a home-grown variety was present to help inspire meaningful worship, so the student, anticipating this, brought a tape-recorded anthem for the special music. He introduced the anthem after the responsive reading but spoke so rapidly I lost much of what he said. It sounded like "Now the Westminster Choir has a selection for us." The tape started and the choir sang. I mused that the Westminster Choir, although renowned, is surely capable of off days. The present number was a prize example of a lapse. After the sermon I learned I misunderstood the preacher's announcement — the selection was a recording effort by a sister church in western Washington County.

I was mightily relieved that I made no discrediting remarks after the service about Westminster Choir's sad decline.

November 26

This past Sunday, the Sunday before Thanksgiving, the student minister at Stockton Springs Community Church preached a sermon on the obligation of all Christians to praise God for their blessings. After the service he presided at a routine meeting of the church's board of trustees and casually announced that one year before, he had preached the same sermon to them word for word. "I don't think you heard what I said the first time," he said artlessly.

This brings up the whole matter, much disputed at gatherings of ministers, about preaching old sermons — sermons that the minister repeats to the same congregation. Some experienced preachers are adamant about never repeating a sermon. My contention is that if a sermon was helpful the first time it was delivered, it is well to use it again, although of course not every six months or even every year. (How little fine music there would be to enjoy if, for example, an orchestra refused to play any of Tschaikovsky's lovely melodies because audiences had heard them before.)

However, I warn the students in preaching classes, never to re-cycle sermons unless those sermons "come alive" to them when they dig them out of their files and read them over. "Don't ever repeat your sermons unless you yourself can glow over them," I urge.

Footnote: Later in the semester in a term paper on preaching, the student minister of the Riverside Church in Vassalboro adopted my advice: "I feel," he wrote, "that I should never preach old sermons of mine unless I can gloat over them."

November 28

About 6:00 a. m. I went out on the porch to get the *News*. The headline that greeted me read: THREE BOYS PERISH IN DEDHAM BLAZE. The front page showed pictures of a house reduced to smoking ruin. The fiery disaster occurred at 7:00 a. m. yesterday morning: Thanksgiving Day.

The pastor of Dedham Church, Jerry Livingston, is a second-year student at the Seminary and has served the church less than three months. Now he must conduct a funeral service for these three little boys — ages eight, six, and two — in the village church tomorrow. He's charged with a responsibility that would try the mettle of a pastor with thirty years' experience. Jerry, who has five little children of his own, may well identify with the stricken father and mother.

He seems to have a sure sense of what to do, although conscious of how little he can really help in the face of the tragedy. Jerry calls at the hospital to see the father, critically burned while trying to rescue his small sons, prays with the mother, and tries to comfort the grandmother and grandfather. He calls me on the phone to say: "I guess I've done all I can before the service; wish I could do more."

A lot of us on the campus who know Jerry well will be thinking of him often before the service tomorrow.

December 1

The North Brewer-Eddington United Methodist Church on Route 9 overlooking the Penobscot River boasts a lively youth fellowship with student Robert Mitchell as its leader. It's a plain-looking white church that sits quietly enough during the week, but awakes to shouts and plenty of teenage yells on Sunday evenings.

Mitchell has a sure touch with teenagers, and has built an attendance from eight youngsters a Sunday evening to over twenty. They like and admire him, but at last night's meeting in the vestry they were noisy and restless. They simply would not settle down: they banged the piano, tossed hymnbooks, wandered about, turned on a portable radio, scribbled notes back and forth, and opened pocketbooks and wallets to show snapshots of their boyfriends and girlfriends.

Mitchell attempted unsuccessfully to gain attention and establish order. In desperation he dismissed them. "You don't want a meeting," he lamented, "so you may as well go home."

Glumly in silence, they filed out. Mitchell collected hymnbooks and a few Bibles, pulled a cover over the piano keys, and snapped shut his briefcase. He was glum and silent, too. He was about to switch off the lights and go out the door when the youngsters began to come back. One by one they re-entered the vestry and began to form a prayer circle. Mitchell, speechless, joined in.

When he got back to the Seminary at 10 p. m. he looked like someone who had spent five days on a cross-country bus, but he was full of good cheer. "You know," he grinned at me, "it's not likely I'll have to put up with another disorderly youth meeting for a long while. Those kids are great."

December 3

This evening I met a pulpit committee in the village of Carthage. The place of meeting, the back room of a small general store, was an unusual setting in which to conduct the King's business. We were surrounded by tins of cat food, cartons of cookies, jars of peanut butter, and bags of Aroostook potatoes. The scribe of the meeting recorded the minutes on an upended oil barrel with a clean newspaper covering the top. The committee got right down to business describing the kind of student minister needed for the village church.

Following the meeting, the chairman of the committee, who is also proprietor of the store, provided refreshments from nearby counters and shelves: cheese, crackers, pickles, ice cream bars, washed down with ginger ale.

Returning to Bangor late at night I successfully (though narrowly) missed a bull moose standing in the middle of Route 2 between Dixfield and Wilton.

I can recall other uncommon places I have met with pulpit committees: in a library reading room, on a street before a Green Front, at the office of the local superintendent of schools, in a restaurant booth, in a firehouse, at a gas station, in a hospital lounge, in a board room of a savings bank, and in a large blue convertible.

December 7

This afternoon I visited the members of three congregations on the "Airline": the East Eddington Community Church, the Clifton Baptist Church, and the Amherst-Aurora Congregational Church. It always seems curious to me, each time I visit these congregations on Route 9, that the three churches sit close to the left-hand side of the road, are painted white, and all have been for years training grounds for future ministers.

By coincidence people in all three called attention to faulty grammar and mispronounciation they hear from their student ministers, either as the students preach or while they make pastoral calls. "Er ... er ... there's one word our student mispronounces over and over again. I've hesitated to speak to him about it, maybe *you'll* speak to him."

Oddly enough, this morning I had heard a student read, from the pulpit of the church he serves, the story of Jesus' birth. The Bible passage tells of the journey of Mary and Joseph to Bethlehem, and says of Joseph, according to the student's unauthorized version, that he went there to be taxed with Mary his *exposed* wife (Luke 2:5). Maybe the student knows better (he

43

should, this particular boner has been around a long while), but there it was, a cause for the congregation to gag or snicker. At any rate, carelessness took over and the student sounded ridiculous. At Sunday dinner the members of the church who attended worship were sure to discuss the blunder, not the message.

Perhaps I should prepare a list of misused and mispronounced words, mimeograph it, and give a copy to each student as a guide for what not to say. The word list would suggest where others have tripped and fallen. It would certainly contain the following, all of which are heard from student pulpits (and alas not from student pulpits only): "pastorial" for pastoral, "submersion" for immersion (particularly painful to Baptist ears), "stanima" for stamina, "dandruff" for dander, "gird up your lions," for gird up your loins, "fractions" for factions, "wench" for winch.

December 8

Today I set off to visit members of the Hiram, Denmark, and Brownfield churches where Harvey Lord is student pastor. The third of these three churches, Brownfield, is less than ten miles from the New Hampshire line and over 150 miles from the Seminary. The drive seems forever. I do it a couple of times a year; Harvey does it every week. I've never heard him grumble about the distance, the zigzagging roads, the frost heaves in the spring, or the potholes all year 'round.

And I've never heard Mrs. Lord complain either. She certainly has every reason to whimper a bit. Now there's a woman who deserves to have a medal pinned to her coat while we all stand at attention.

Harvey studies at school all week, drives home on Friday afternoon, and sees his family only a few moments before he's off to make calls. He can spend little time with them on weekends. The sick, the shut-ins, the hospitalized require his pastoral attention. His wife is sometimes lonely because she sees so little of her husband even during the weekends. Good humoredly she tries to make the most of her weekend opportunities to see him. Lately, she and the children have bundled themselves into the family car to ride with Harvey while he makes his rounds.

When I dropped by the parsonage today for coffee, after visiting several members of the congregations, I was prepared to be compassionate. I expected she might be resentful that in order to visit with her husband she had to sit patiently in a cold car on rural roads with restless children. When I opened my mouth to offer sympathy she brought me up short. "Riding around the countryside with Harvey isn't all that bad," she smiled, "the kids and I have become experts at word games and roadside cribbage."

December 9

I've been out often on the "Airline" this fall. (Route 9 has this name, I guess, because it is the most direct way to Calais. It is hardly straight, however.) The drive today to visit a member of one of the roadside churches was pleasant, and it seemed more like Indian summer than Christmas carol time. It was hard to believe our local weather specialist when he said this

45

morning that the temperature would plummet to zero tomorrow.

I found the church sexton in his backyard chopping fireplace wood. He sat on the chopping block, and took pot shots at the ladies' sewing circle — no longer, he claims, as useful as it should be. The members are not getting along together. The woodsplitter's wife is in "The Circle," so he has the inside story.

He told me there are six women "in the crew" and three of them want to be "boss." Three to supervise, three to do the work. "My wife," he said, running a testing finger down the axe blade, "comes home from circle meetings and gobbles tranquilizers. Every Sunday the young student preacher at the church prays for peace to come to the whole world; he'd better start ter home and pray that these women right here'll quit their quarreling."

December 11

Boswell reports Samuel Johnson saying, "Sir, a woman's preaching is like a dog walking on his hind legs. It is not done well, but you are surprised to find it done at all." Johnson would wonder at the number of women occupying pulpits these days and indeed would be surprised that so many are doing it well. Seldom is there a class in preaching at theological seminaries now that does not include at least four or five women. A recent religious publication reports that in some seminaries as many as forty percent of the students enrolled in classes are women.

They will have a hard time getting placed in pulpits,

because the prejudice still lingers among Maine churches that a man who is a dull preacher is more acceptable as a minister than a woman who is eloquent. Every so often some church member — usually a woman — will say to me: "I don't know what it is, but there's something about a woman in the pulpit that goes against my grain."

Usually, the search committee of a congregation looking for a minister to fill its vacant pulpit will be composed of more women than men. If an effective woman minister lets it be known that she is interested in being considered for the opening, the women on the committee will become really vocal. One female member is likely to say: "Women ministers are well and good, and I don't have a thing against them, but we certainly don't care to have one for *this* church, the men of the church just wouldn't stand for a woman preacher."

Male members of the committee say little or nothing at all. (If they agree with the female committee member, they'll be labeled male chauvinists; if they speak in favor of women preachers, they'll arouse the wrath of the women on the committee who themselves do not want any lady minister.)

Now and then, however, a church will give me a glad surprise by accepting a woman student minister. Three weeks ago the rough and ready chairman of the Hampden Congregational Church pulpit committee asked me for the names of candidates for the vacant pulpit of his church. I suggested three: two men and a woman. The three had already enjoyed a satisfactory experience as student pastors.

47

"Can't you give me the name of one more man?" the chairman asked. "This church will never in the world take a woman for a minister, no matter how good she is."

"But you haven't heard this one," I replied. "She really is a topnotch preacher; why not give her a chance? All I ask is that she get a fair hearing along with the two men."

"Won't do a mite of good," he said, "the congregation here'll never put up with a pulpit pounder in petticoats."

I let this pass, feeling he was not really up to date, but kept pressing him to give student Irene Edman an opportunity to be heard. Finally he gave in, agreed to listen to her, and promised to arrange for other committee members to hear her. "But," he persisted, "it's just a waste of time, I'm going along with you just to keep you happy."

The chairman kept his word, took his committee out to the Monroe Community Church where Mrs. Edman was preaching. That did it. She was invited by a unanimous committee to preach in the Hampden church as a candidate and received the call to become the new minister.

Immediately the chairman reported to me the action taken by the church: "Hey," he yelled over the phone, "why didn't you *tell* me she was that good in the pulpit?"

December 15

I'm completely mystified by the reaction of Gordon

48

and Betty Richardson to the preaching of two supply student ministers in the coastal town of Stonington. These two devoted lay people have listened to scores of preachers in their day, and for years have been key people in the United Methodist Church, where Gordon has been lay leader.

The first young preacher they heard was a senior: smooth, well tailored, and labeled by his classmates and professors as "sophisticated." He has even had a poem published! The second substitute student preacher was a sophomore with rough edges, a halting style, and a nondescript presence. He can't even *quote* a poem of any length.

Gordon and Betty reported to me on both students' speaking and conduct of worship. Their evaluation floored me. "This second preacher must be farther advanced in his studies than the one we heard the week before."

My word! When a prosy sophomore who has taken no courses in theology, Christian history, and Bible, out-performs a senior who has won the respect of his professors and has passed complicated courses in divinity, I'm left puzzling about just what's getting done in classrooms and the lecture hall at our Seminary.

December 16

"I suppose we could do a lot worse," is the way a member of the Danforth Methodist Church described his feelings about the present student pastor leadership. Then he adds: "The preacher we've got is about as good as we can expect to get for the money we pay."

This unenthusiastic evaluation was echoed by several other members I visited. The Danforth people were bitterly disappointed in two previous ministers who served the church full-time.

The first minister worked with the people a little over a year, then suddenly left town. One Sunday morning he did not arrive at church to conduct worship. The parsonage is only a short distance from the church; after ten minutes with no minister appearing, a member of the official board left the waiting congregation, crossed to the parsonage, and found a message from the pastor tacked to the outside of the kitchen door: "When you find this note I'll be gone; I just can't stand this town any longer."

The next minister stayed a little longer, but left town for a new job as a beer salesman. He soon appeared in the area pushing his product with more energy than he ever showed in church work — much to the embarrassment of temperance-minded Methodists.

The plight of this church, and so many like it, in not finding dedicated, effective leadership, is heartrending. Floundering churches in larger centers can combine with more flourishing ones, but countless congregations in many of Maine's remote areas do not have others to combine with.

December 18

An irresistible urge to burst into print may explain why so many student ministers publish parish newsletters. They no sooner settle into a parsonage than they seize the crank of a duplicating machine to issue bulletins to be mailed to all church members. This is a good idea, I suppose, but students know I favor investing their scanty time in more vital work: in Christian education, for example, or in sermon preparation or pastoral calling. So I'm seldom shown their news sheets.

But this morning I found stuffed into my Seminary mailbox a four-page newsletter published by the student pastor of a Hancock County church. The news item that caught my eye advertised two outstanding features of next Sunday's morning service. It read: "The wife of the pastor will sing a solo." "Living Through a Trying Experience" was the minister's sermon title.

December 19

The student pastors' efforts to involve Maine countryside congregations in formal worship are often carried too far. But students are not really to be blamed for seeking to keep abreast of changing liturgical patterns. Meeting houses where twenty-five, even ten years ago, a lighted candle, an impressive cross, a split chancel were abominations, now often include one or all of these appointments.

In some churches, where student ministers have introduced formal worship aids, little boys or girls dressed in white gowns have been selected to walk down the center aisle, light candles at the beginning of worship, then extinguish them at the end.

One Seminary professor, Dr. Stephen Szikszai, who supplies many wayside pulpits in Maine, is often beguiled by the worship ways of churches. Last Sunday he filled in for the student pastor who serves the

Canaan Community Church. No cute little acolyte was available to light the candles for the opening of the meeting. After a brief delay a strapping trustee was pressed into service as a substitute. He proceeded gravely down the center aisle, approached the table on which there was a substantial brass cross flanked by two white candles. Obviously he was a most efficient person who believed in wasting no motions. He bowed low before the cross while standing on one foot, struck a big wooden match on the other, and lighted the candles. He bowed again, this time with both feet on the floor, then solemnly retreated up the aisle to a rear pew.

The incongruity of the balancing act with a deep ceremonial bow and the exploding match was seemingly lost on all but the visiting preacher who rose and announced the opening hymn: "Let There Be Light, Lord God of Hosts."

December 20

Up to now I have not been able to place student Ronald Perry in a church as a part-time pastor. He does not "come on strong" in the pulpit and hardly sparkles when he meets people.

He does want desperately to have a chance to go to work, but the right opening has yet to present itself. Two reasons are behind his eagerness for placement: he genuinely wants to serve God in a parish; he's down to his last twenty dollars. He told me he may have to leave school unless he gets an opportunity to serve a church which will provide a parsonage and at least thirty-five dollars a week. I've been seeking a place for him in eastern Washington County; so far without success. But now has come the prospect of an opening near Bangor.

Today, Perry dropped by to learn whether I had any encouragement for him. I assured him that I thought he would soon be placed. Overjoyed he promised to work his heart out as a student minister.

He said that he and his mother who keeps house for him have been living "mostly on baked beans" for a month and are getting tired of the diet. Last week he took his mother to a public supper at the local YMCA, thinking the change would do her good. The main item on the menu was baked beans.

December 23

People in Maine parishes often tell me they are forever being surprised by many examples of Seminary students' freeheartedness. Sometimes students bicker, quarrel, snipe at one another, and harbor hostile feelings. All these students are human; few are candidates for sainthood. But again and again to my office come stories of true friendship that make me suck in my breath. Christmas spirit is here for sure.

Student William Heinrick was to preach in Perry, Meddybemps, and Dennysville last Sunday. He got into an automobile collision the night before he was to fill the assignment. He dragged back into Bangor late Saturday night, needing a substitute for the following morning engagements. Fellow student Robert Sargent quietly offered to go, although he had preached a sermon only once in his life. He had to drive a total of 250 miles in a none-too-reliable car for a very modest stipend. He got up at 4 a. m. on Sunday, drove to the villages, and conducted worship in each. On return his only comment was: "The third time I delivered the sermon I knew it pretty well."

The year-round Christmas spirit of students is not reserved just for other members of the Seminary family. Often I hear from church members how student ministers serve their parishioners in unexpectedly compassionate ways.

The latest example of warmheartedness reported to me comes from a Hampden church where Quentin Peacock is pastor. Peacock has no car (he sometimes borrows one to make distant hospital calls), so he visits mostly on foot. He is one of the most consistently compassionate of student ministers. A crippled girl of twelve is his special pastoral concern right now. Although she lives over a mile from the center of town, people often see the young minister pushing her in a wheelchair through the village on Saturdays in late spring, summer, and fall.

With snow already a foot and a half deep this winter, Peacock just may put runners on the wheelchair so he can fetch his young charge to town to see the Christmas lights.

December 25

How better to observe Christmas than by going to church? Part of the day with the family, part of the day in church — that seems to me about the right balance for celebrating Jesus' birth.

54

So I took a snowy drive through Newport, Palmyra, Canaan, Skowhegan, and Norridgewock to Mercer. (Sibley Pond that sprawls between Palmyra and Canaan on Route 2 was frozen solid. A solitary pickerel fisherman was sitting on a keg of some kind watching his tip-ups. The snow was blowing around him but he seemed not to want a hut for protection. He lifted his hand when I slowed on the bridge to look at him. I don't care a hang for ice fishing but just seeing a line dropped through a hole in the ice made me hanker for flower-carpeted hillsides, open lakes, and rushing brooks.)

Bob Dobson, a Seminary junior, is pastor of the United Methodist Church in Mercer; he was standing in the drive when I got there. When I stepped inside the rather plain sanctuary I counted fourteen for the afternoon service, and every last member of that congregation sang! It was a marvelous sight, and extremely unusual.

In most churches there are worshipers who hold a hymnbook but do not sing; others hold a hymnbook and religiously make their mouths go even though carrying a tune is for them impossible. (All honor to them.) Still others do not try to sing, nor even hold a book; such folk simply stand and clutch the back of the pew in front of them. They stare at the communion table, the front wall, or the preacher; they are just waiting to sit down.

In Mercer everybody sang. Four men were present, including a young serviceman in uniform, and *he* sang well, sharing a hymnbook with an eleven-year-old boy. The piano clanged along out of tune.

The pianist sang — also out of tune. But everybody sang!

Glory to God in the highest!

January 5

"You've got to get this fellow out of here. Attendance is down, the organist has quit, and the offerings have dropped to almost nothing — and it's all because of that student you sent us for a pastor. He's a good enough guy I guess but he sure doesn't fit around here. With that stable of preachers you've got at the Seminary why in the world did you send us such a dud?"

(This is the gist of a phone call from a vexed layman. It's Monday morning, 7:30. I wonder why bad news arrives on wings Monday morning, while good news about student ministers' work limps in about Thursday afternoon.) The big question for me to answer about this layman's complaint: is he mad because he got his nose tweaked by the student preacher's Sunday sermon and needs to yell about it a little; or, is the student really a pathetic flop in his service to the church?

Another congregation is also on my mind this morning. According to several reports from a church in Sagadahoc County the members are not happy with the minister; the minister is not happy with the members. Because the congregation and the minister cannot seem to pull together, the church people wish he would leave, and he, oh so much, wants to go! But right now this poor guy with four children can't find another congregation that wants him.

Last week I heard an account from a member of

the New Sharon Congregational Church about how —
many years ago — it set up a safeguard against getting misfits as ministers. The congregation had endured the services of three inept pastors in a row and
was not about to put up with a fourth — at least for
long. In case they got a dud in the next parson they
determined to use the freeze play. This bright idea
came to a member of the trustee board which met one
evening to talk about a new heating unit needed for the
parsonage. "Let's wait," he said, "until the new
minister has been here a while. If we like him we'll
put in the furnace, if we don't we'll just freeze him
out."

January 6

Always the unusual!

Parsons who are in close touch with Maine people
need never succumb to boredom: church members and
local citizens will provide sufficient special and extra-
ordinary requests to keep the days lively for any minister.

Today I heard of a request not often made of a
Protestant pastor. Burton Bartholomew, serving his
first parish, at Holden, recently conducted the funeral
service of a man who was a Protestant but whose wife
is a Roman Catholic. The evening before the funeral
the student called on the widow to express his concern
and to enquire about her wishes regarding the service
to be held at two the following afternoon.

He was met by an appeal from the widow that
brought out his sympathy and sensitivity. She asked,
"May I call you 'Father' just for this evening and to-

57

morrow when the service will be held? You see, it will be from you that I shall draw support and help."

The student, although Protestant to the core, readily complied with her request. Later, the widow remarked to an acquaintance about the gracious helpfulness of the pastor who was a "Father" for parts of two days.

January 8

Last Sunday ten sermons were preached at the First Parish Church of York. Five minutes were allotted to members of the youth group of the church to speak to the adult congregation at the morning service. The "sermonettes" were titled "What the Christian Faith Means to Me," and were delivered in observance of Youth Sunday.

In the vestry, just before the service, the group clustered about the youth minister. (The term youth "leader" or youth "worker" is no longer an acceptable title to those engaged in this enterprise.) Eveline Smith, in charge of the group and a junior at the Seminary, felt the young people needed powerful support for what was ahead. The teenagers did, too. They were not only nervous about speaking in public, they were downright scared. Just before filing into the sanctuary to take their places behind the pulpit one of them stammered, "I think . . we'd better pray."

The youth minister travels 165 miles from Bangor to the York Church each weekend to provide supervision and friendship for these youngsters, who on this particular Sunday, in spite of their fears, won the attention of the congregation. One elderly deacon, after the service, was heard to remark, "With all that young talent around here maybe we can let our regular preacher go."

Mrs. Smith, mother of four, and the foster mother of eight orphaned teens she and her husband Jim took into their home, will some day become a full-time pastor. After graduation from the Seminary, and following ordination, she will enjoy a sense of accomplishment.

But such a feeling of achievement will not be more pronounced to her than that Youth Sunday when ten teenage preachers gathered about her for encouragement and support. These days Evie Smith has plenty to think about on her long weekend drives on Interstate 95.

January 12

A young Seminary junior yesterday supplied the pulpit of a small village church on Sandy River near Farmington. The student is especially wide-awake to Maine's natural wonders and when he arrived back at school he commented to me that Sandy River was appropriately named. "Most of the time," he said, "when I caught sight of it on my way to and from the church I noticed that sand is more often visible than rocks."

The student's quality of alertness was not only evident when it came to nature, he was also sensitive to the people he met at the church. When he entered the sanctuary well before the service he was met by a solicitous deacon who kindly interpreted the order of worship for him. He incidentally warned the young preacher that a certain ancient member of the fellowship who regularly attends services had a "heart condition." He cautioned that the ailing man might be prostrated if anything said in the sermon should evoke hearty laughter. After the brief conversation with the deacon, the student retired to the rest room, where he hastily overhauled his sermon notes and struck out a humorous anecdote.

That young preacher's sensitivity will enable him to become a resourceful minister.

January 13

Last night I received a phone call from the Milbridge United Church of Christ. The members highly approve of the present student minister.

A few years ago the congregation was not pleased at all with the pastor who was serving them at the time. That young fellow was articulate, sophisticated, and intelligent — but slipping in his studies: his record of grades showed three "Ds" in one semester. The Seminary dean commented in a faculty meeting, "It's my guess this guy is putting in too much work in the church he serves, not enough time on his courses." The faculty agreed and volunteered several relevant comments about the student's addiction to late papers and frequent class absences.

I called on members of the Milbridge Church, the next day, expecting to find the young man presiding over a flourishing endeavor. First I visited David Kennedy, a member of the Church's official board, who was also prominent in Maine's Legislative Assembly. Kennedy, however, diplomatic in Maine politics, is always quick to lay it on the line when evaluating the work of student ministers. While he chewed on a strong cigar, I said: "Dave, we at the Seminary have the impression that your minister must be doing a tremendous job in church work — his Seminary studies are slipping." Kennedy said: "We in town have been thinking that he must be doing a tremendous job in his Seminary classes — he isn't doing anything here."

January 16

With some reluctance I set off for Princeton in a snowstorm thinking I might be in for a wild trip. Jim Bigney, the Channel 2 weather specialist, forecast *flurries,* but I'm never quite sure of Jim's predictions.

Three options are open for the traveler from Bangor headed for Princeton: 1. You can drive to Ellsworth, then follow Route 1 through Machias and Calais to Princeton — 170 miles; 2. You can attempt the Airline which is rough, crooked, and narrow — 100 miles; 3. You can try the Lincoln and Topsfield way — 130 miles.

Choosing the last route I set off in lightly falling snow at 3 p. m. to meet the pulpit committee of the Princeton Congregational Church. By the time I arrived in Princeton the snow was "heavy," but momentarily I forgot about getting home while meeting with the committee in a small lunch room where English muffins and hot coffee were served.

At 7:30 p. m. I set out for Bangor and the fun began. Already eight to eleven inches of snow had fallen on the highway, which was unplowed and so white I could not determine with certainty where the shoulders were. Although managing to stay on the road I used an hour and a half getting up Route 1 to Topsfield — only twenty miles had been covered on the trip home, hardly a beginning. I began to wish I'd accepted the kind invitation of the Princeton folk to stay with them all night.

A glance at my road map gave me plenty of uneasiness. From Topsfield west to Lincoln is a forty-one mile swing of lonely, risky driving, so I sat in the car waiting for a plow to come through. I'd follow that. At last one did appear, and I fell in behind. The trouble was the plow quit half-way across the forty-one mile stretch.

By now the temperature was minus four and the snow one and a half feet deep. Some faint wheel tracks meant that possibly another plow had gone through ahead, perhaps an hour before; so I gripped the wheel and started off. After about a dozen miles I went into a spin, sliding into a big, soft snowbank at the bottom of a hill. Stuck. The time was 2 a. m., and I was feeling low.

After fifteen minutes of futile digging behind my rear wheels I just sat for a while. All at once a driver in a pickup truck zigzagged down the hill toward me, coming from Lincoln. He stopped, got out, swore loudly and eloquently at the continuing snowstorm, the absence of plowmen, and damn fool drivers who didn't know enough to stay home in blizzards. Putting his truck to work, he pulled me onto the road, informing me that he'd been playing poker with some guys in Lincoln. He surely dealt *me* a good hand.

At 3 a. m. I reached Lincoln and Bangor at 4:45 —

after nearly ten hours of skidding and sliding one hundred and thirty miles through one of weatherman Jim Bigney's snow flurries.

But just the same, it was fun. Sitting out there with snow falling all about, making the firs and spruces sag across the road until they touched one another in great white arches — well, I liked the softness and the quiet.

January 19

Loneliness is the bane of many student pastors' wives. One wife living most of the week in a Franklin County parish without her husband, who is away at school, is especially forlorn. The student has told me, half seriously, too, "The wife gets so lonely sometimes, she calls up the local telephone operator just to hear her say, 'Number, please'."

Growing some, but not half fast enough, is the concern of church people for the upkeep of parsonages. It always seems that the parsonage is the draftiest house in the parish. I remember a particularly well-ventilated one in Piscataquis County, heated by a sawdust burner, that was never warm. One day I found the student's wife sitting at the top of the hallway stairs mending socks. She explained: "Up here is the warmest place in the house."

January 20

A report came today from a little church on the Airline that the student pastor is doing great work. In other days the church has known low moments: spotty attendance, little in the offering plates, and general apathy. The work is now flourishing with a lively church school. I recall when no parents could be found in town who would build a fire in winter so that children could meet in the building. Parents were unconcerned about their children receiving Bible instruction.

I can't help wondering how many of the same parents wrote indignant "letters to the editor" complaining about the United States Supreme Court ruling which eliminated devotional Bible reading in public schools.

January 21

Donald Elliot is the student pastor at the Eaton, Weston, and Danforth Methodist Churches. Heavy snow made him twenty minutes late last Sunday for the service at the smallest of the three. He arrived to find the church door locked, but he noticed that the path was shoveled and smoke was rising from the chimney. After a few minutes of speculation on the whereabouts of the congregation, Elliot drove down one of the roads leading from the church. Around a turn he caught up with four people trudging through the snow; he had found his congregation: two women, one man, and a boy of thirteen. Elliot asked, "Do you still want a service?" They did. All climbed into his car and plowed back to the church. One woman produced a key for the door, another played the organ, the man put another log into the stove, and the boy passed the offering plate.

It's not the only church in the Maine countryside where the congregation is so small that it can get into one car, and where every member attending has a job.

All ministers who conduct worship at least forty-eight Sundays a year have to resist the temptation to rely on threadbare phrases. Every student minister, after being in a parish for only a few Sundays, faces the danger of using moth-eaten expressions at announcement time, in giving out hymn numbers, and of course while preaching and praying.

Worshipers in student-led parishes enjoy renewing acquaintances each Sunday in Church, but increasingly kick to me about old friends they encounter there in the form of mildewed expressions.

One tried expression which is irking listeners in several parishes is: "Let us confess our sins to Almighty God." "Sure, we need to do this," complain the church-goers, "but does the minister have to use exactly the same phrase *every* Sunday? Can't he change the wording a little? Can't he call sins 'iniquities,' or 'transgressions,' or 'unrighteousness' or *something* else?"

The above formula is not the only repetitive utterance annoying worshipers. A few years back, the Frankfort church people complained that the pastor spent too little time preparing his pulpit prayers. They said he fell back repeatedly on seedy phrases. In fact, members of the church quoted to me one he used every Sunday: "O God, bless this church set in the midst of the perplexities of a changing universe." A mother of four, always in church with her children, called on her youngest boy to ask the blessing one night at supper. While all heads were bowed, the little fellow recited in a monotone: "O God, bless this house set in the midst of the perplexities of a changing universe."

Students who attend chapel regularly at the Seminary with their ears open may hear a few of their professors' ever recurring upliftings. In fact, observing students conduct worship in their parishes, I often discover their teachers' prayer cliches have been borrowed by the students. Some of these shopworn supplications the student-served congregations listen to Sunday after Sunday are:

"O God, speak to us the word we need to hear."

"O Thou, whom no man hath seen at any time."

"Direct us, O Lord, in all our doings with thy most gracious favor."

"Almighty God, who art more ready to hear than we to pray."

"O God, we thank you for your grace that has sustained us in the past."

Watered-down, or doctored-up thoughts from their classroom lecture notes are sometimes employed by students as filler material in the sermons they preach to their own congregations on Sundays. Probably the professors would be flattered by seeing mimeographed copies of their ideas produced in student-led services, but they would be less than pleased to see students aping professorial mannerisms and awkward gestures.

January 26

Coming out of the Hammond Street United Church of Christ after the last Bangor Seminary Convocation lecture of the afternoon, I met student minister Richard Dale on the steps. Dale was electrified by the spirited singing of the large congregation which attended the Beach Quiet Hour, but mournful about the apathetic singing in the church he serves, both by the small choir and the small congregation. "I'm having real choir trouble," he groaned. "I wish I could get some young people to sing in it. It's made up of one trustee, three members of the business committee, and one prima donna, and," he went on, "not one of 'em can sing, but all suffer from delusions of adequacy."

My sympathies were aroused for him in his troubles. Music in the small church is often pitiable: either the choir wallops away at anthems miles beyond them, or a seedy soloist oversings some simple gospel song. Fortunate is the student pastor if he combines sound musical judgment with a clear singing voice of his own — just as Ray Hollis does who is pastor of the North Searsport Methodist Church.

Hollis is one of the finest singers among our Seminary students, and the people in his church are much blessed by his talent. One Sunday I visited his church to observe him conduct worship. During the service Hollis, twenty-two years old, sang, "Our God, Our Help In Ages Past" with a man, seventy-two. I watched them stand together on a tiny platform, the one dark-haired and young, the other white-haired and old. The touching contrast was not lost on several members of the congregation whose eyes grew a bit damp as the couple sang again, this time the old favorite, "Abide With Me."

January 28

The last Convocation lecture was over at noon today. What a sunburst of luminaries were present to enlighten and inspire: Paul Tillich, Howard Thurman, and Perry Miller!

The pastors from churches all over the U. S. have started back to their parishes; the lecturers, clutching their generous honoraria, have taken off from Bangor International; the alumni have said their goodbyes to one another with promises to meet again next January; the students, some enthralled, some befuddled, have turned back to the classroom; and the professors have scrambled up the hill to their offices to "get in" their last semester's grades.

What of the lay people who attended? I have a hunch that little of the lectures got across to them — not because they are one whit stupid, but because the great chunks of jargon shot from the platform pass high over their heads.

Every year it's the same story. The Seminary president and dean push hard at faculty meetings to invite at least one out of three lecturers who will especially appeal to the average lay person and the average minister, who are not wholly familiar with a complicated theological vocabulary. They seldom gain their point.

One lay person from the Milford United Church of Christ was not excited about last year's Convocation presentations. His student minister, Ernest Huntzinger, asked him whether he found the speakers inspiring. The man replied: "The first one I think I might have understood if I could have heard him better; the second I could hear but couldn't understand; the third, uh, uh, well, I sort of quit on him and slipped downtown to a movie."

For thirty-five years I have attended annual convocations, twenty-two as a member of the faculty, thirteen as a Maine pastor. I always find lay members of churches, who do attend, alive to challenging ideas if they can hear and if they can understand.

January 29

Public spirited students sometimes undertake peculiar tasks in towns where they serve.

David Smith, pastor of the Congregational Church in Eastport, was unhappy about the town clock in the church steeple; it was seldom running. He expressed his feelings at a church meeting one evening: "Our clock is a landmark and should be telling time. It's not a good advertisement for our church or for Eastport to have a clock that is not working."

He was told that nobody in town was willing to wind it regularly. Dissatisfied with this nonsolution, Smith volunteered to wind it himself. So Monday mornings before he returns to school for the week he lugs a huge iron crank up the stairs of the bell tower and winds and winds. Returning Friday noon from Seminary classes, he again shoulders the crank and winds some more. He acknowledges that on zero days in December, January, February, and sometimes March, when the wind is blowing hard off Passamaquoddy Bay, he wishes he had been less insistent about keeping the clock running. The belfry climb provides a beguiling view in summer, but an endurance test in winter.

Not only do students engage in exceptional tasks for the public, occasionally they have remarkable chores thrust upon them by individuals. An example was reported to me recently by Robert Hatfield, who is serving the Hartland Methodist Church. An ancient lady in the parish invited him to dinner and, as payment for the delicious meal, insisted that he listen to her play the piano for an hour. While she provided the recital he was expected to sit upon a sofa in the living room adjoining the "studio." (Hatfield acclaims her cooking but is less than inspired by her musicianship.) Sitting on a sofa after a hearty meal is conducive to sleep, but his napping was repeatedly interrupted by the lady appearing in the doorway expectant of applause.

The "speak-out" is another chore for some student ministers in towns where they serve churches. The Grange supper, the women's group luncheon, the basketball banquet, the dedication of a youth recreation center, the high school assembly exercises — all of these call upon a student's talents who is supposed to provide the appropriate words for just any type of gathering. Sometimes student ministers are a bit rebellious about taking on these time-consuming assignments. (In honesty, though, many of them might confess they had rather go about making speeches than study for a Greek exam.)

A Seminary senior was invited to speak at a Tranquility Grange supper this past Saturday in Lincolnville Center where he is pastor. He did it. But he beefed to me about it this morning. Said he: "I ate a supper I didn't need so I could get up and tell a lot of stories I couldn't remember to a bunch of Grangers who'd heard them all before. If those people down there weren't the salt of the earth I'd never have done it."

January 30

"We need a *young* minister to work with our youth."

So many times I have heard this statement. Some member of a pulpit committee in search of a new pastor is sure to emphasize the word "young." But I've known several ministers of twenty-five who were all crossed up with their teenage groups, while other pastors of forty-five have gotten on fine with them. Boys and girls couldn't care less about a leader's age. Some of the most effective church school teachers I know are elderly. Age has not one thing to do with being accepted by youth.

This fact was made vivid in a Machias church. Fifteen teenage boys in church school were clamoring for a regular teacher. The school's superintendent, with no success, scoured the membership roster of the church to discover a young layman or a young couple to teach the class. At last a sixty-year-old retired elementary school teacher unexpectedly responded to the need. "I'll give it a try," she promised. The student pastor of the church, teaching a junior high class himself, was astounded by the lady's daring. He was doubtful of the result, but applauded her dedication and hoped for the best.

Two years later the lady was still teaching the class

which had swelled to twenty, and the young fellows nominated her the best teacher in Washington County.

January 31

Once I heard about a course offered at a certain school of pharmacy called Pharmaceutical Incompatibilities. The course was about substances that won't ordinarily mix.

Some sad incompatibles take place in my work. Every now and then a group of church people and a student pastor simply do not mix. The student is eager to serve the church well, and the congregation is made up of cooperative people. This should be a good blend, but somehow right from the start the minister and the people don't get along; they're not meant for each other.

The student wants the church to grow in all ways (so do the people) but he "comes on too fast," and the church people are more deliberate in thought and action. The student favors a certain type of hymn sung in worship; the congregation prefers another kind. The student wants the offering to follow the sermon; the congregation desires that it precede the sermon. He prefers not to wear a pulpit gown; the people think it adds dignity to the service and request him to wear one. (If he pleads, "A gown's more than I can afford right now," the church business committee meets, goes into action, plans a public supper, raises ninety-five dollars, and buys a gown. Now he has to wear it; the people are very proud of it.)

In some parishes it seems as though congregation and minister are barreling down opposite sides of the street. I don't always know how I can be helpful to a mismatched church and student, or how to win a gold medal as a peacemaker. I may have a cup of coffee with the student and mention to him the virtue of patience, urging him to go slowly and win the confidence of the people. (Many students break into wide grins when I counsel patience, they've heard me on this subject before.) I also talk with members of the congregation and ring the changes on the *same* word. No grin comes from the people, just a deep collective sigh, "We *have* been patient."

Consecrated patience, I really do believe, is the ingredient that will bring these two into harmony. Most students find quickly how to work with church people, and seek to lead rather than to drive. One of the first non-academic lessons a divinity student learns is that shoving the throttle to the floor too soon in a church is usually countered by church officials jamming on the brakes. In the duel between throttle and brakes the brakes win. For their part most church members understand that a student has much to learn, and they study how to work with him.

Occasionally incompatibles remain incompatibles. A while back the Oxford County United Parish was the scene of acute dissimilarity between the minister and the congregation. The fine church people had a hard-working student but repeated collisions of the pastor's *wills* and the people's *won'ts* finally showed the partnership had to be dissolved. After the young man resigned and announced his impending departure, the good people of the parish arranged a farewell party attended by a host of well-wishers. The student

73

was overwhelmed by this display of affection and esteem by former "foes."

I am happy to report that the Oxford County United Parish and their new minister got along just fine, and that the young man who left, eventually went to a parish where he and his congregation hit it off very well.

February 2

Late this afternoon a student signaled to me from the library reading room that he wanted a conference. I always enjoy talking with him about his parish experiences. He grabbed a cup of coffee from the Canteen and sat down in the office. Almost always he is casually although neatly dressed, but today he showed up in a dark suit and conservative necktie.

I think of him as one of our coolest and most self-possessed student ministers. Today, despite his subdued attire, he looked a bit hassled.

He reported that he had just lived through the most embarrassing moment of his life. A couple of hours before our conversation he had conducted a funeral service in his church for a prominent member. While relatives and friends gathered for the service just before two o'clock a drunk slipped unnoticed into a pew.

The service began and after reading several Bible passages the student spoke of Jesus' resurrection: "Jesus rose from the dead. His body did not lie in the tomb seven years, it did not lie in the tomb seven months, it did not lie in the tomb even seven days . . ." At that moment the drunk jumped up suddenly.

"I know, I know," he yelled, "*three* days, *three* days!"

The mourners were horrified, the funeral director was dismayed, the student minister was silenced; but the drunk was much satisfied with himself and the situation.

I asked the student how he rescued the service from such a dilemma. "Well," he said, "the poor guy, having clinched the matter, weaved down the aisle to the back of the church and left. I wasn't at all sure what to do — but I decided I'd better end the service; so, I pronounced the benediction."

The young parson, fortunately, did not ask me what I would have done had I been conducting the service. The fact is, I think he did it about right.

February 3

Today, I drove through rain, sleet, snow, slush, fog, sand, and salt to a church in Franklin County. I felt sorry for myself; the tricky weather got to me. But I'm only bound to drive over there occasionally, while the student who serves the church I visited has to do it once a week, sometimes twice. Icy roads and blizzards have not kept him from spending each weekend, this tough winter, calling on the sick, leading Sunday worship, meeting with committees, and directing a youth choir.

Several people I visited seemed unfriendly to the student although no specific complaints were expressed about his work. A comment made by a certain church member startled me: "After this student is finished here we're not going to have another;

75

we're through subsidizing the education of divinity students."

The church is well over one hundred miles from the Seminary. The student must pay his travel expense and get his own meals on a salary of thirty-five dollars for the weekend.

Some subsidy!

The contrast is most vivid between the attitude of that less-than-generous-hearted Christian and the attitude of a certain lay person from one of the churches ministered to by Dr. Margaret Hendricksen of *Seven Steeples* fame. Dr. Hendricksen, recently on vacation, asked me to send a supply preacher in her absence to occupy her pulpits. I sent a very young man — only twenty-one — to fill in for her. The youthfulness of the boy touched the hearts of several members of the congregation; they observed that on a very cold and snowy day he had no overshoes or hat.

Monday morning when the young fellow was back at the Seminary he was called on the phone and invited to lunch by a lay person (on a business trip to Bangor) who had heard him preach the day before. After lunch the church member asked the student to accompany him to a men's furnishing store in Bangor; there he outfitted the boy with a suit, two shirts, ties, overshoes, an overcoat, and a hat.

As they say, "It takes all kinds."

February 5

One of the most lively parishes served by students is on Route 2 in the town of Milford. The white church, sitting close to the highway, about a mile north of the Old Town bridge, has been a training ground for countless men and women seminarians.

The members of the church whom I visited recently are satisfied that they are being led by a conscientious preacher. Dick Douglas, a deacon of the fellowship who is a bank official in Bangor, filled me in on what he thinks of the boy: "I predict that our pastor will become one of the best speakers we've ever heard — and we've sure had a lot of them from your local 'preacher factory'."

This seemed to be the consensus of the congregation. Some discerning people are listening to that young man every Sunday.

My curiosity aroused, I invited the Milford pastor to come by my office for a chat. I thought I might get some clues about why he is such a promising speaker. He hustled in today carrying a "special" sermon for me to read and evaluate. He is always keen to talk about sermon preparation and delivery.

In our conversation he declared that sometimes when he prepares a sermon he preaches three. First he prepares one at his desk: thinking, reading, consulting different versions of the Bible, examining commentaries, and writing it all out. Then he types the completed sermon. But when he stands behind the pulpit facing the congregation, he often gets the feeling that the sermon he has painstakingly prepared is all wrong; so he pushes it under the pulpit and improvises another — instantaneously! This is the second one. Finally, late Sunday night he levels at his roommate what he really meant to say, and that, he concludes, is the best of the three. "What a pity," he commented to me, "that the congregation to hear my best effort is composed of only one sleepyhead!"

February 10

Many church members' sense of propriety might be offended if they knew how some student weekend supply preachers, non-owners of automobiles, get to their Sunday preaching appointments.

A lady member of the Limington Congregational Church called me last week, "Will you send us a student 'fill-in' for Sunday? We have no one to preach for us." I agreed to find one, but before starting the search I studied the road map taped to a wall in my office. Limington is at least 135 miles from the Seminary. No student owning a car was available, so the supply pastor would need to ride the bus to Portland, and, if possible, catch another bus from Portland to the church.

After I coaxed him a bit, Paul Paskewitz agreed to fill in. I warned him of the transportation problem and of the modest honorarium: "Fourteen dollars and a warm dinner" (to quote the promise of the Limington lady who had telephoned). Although Paul was persuaded to go, he was dismayed to find bus fare more than the "salary."

Sunday morning, at six o'clock, the Seminary's Old Testament professor looked out the window of his apartment and saw Paul on Hammond Street, thumb poised, ready to go preach the gospel whenever a kind driver would give him a lift.

He actually did make Limington on time!

Also, last week, telephone calls registering distress came from two churches in Aroostook County: one call was from Hodgdon, the other from Monticello. Both churches are members of the Methodist Conference of Maine. The regular minister who serves both was ill, and a substitute speaker was needed. With some relief I noted that even though twenty miles apart one student could fill both pulpits because of different service times. I called on Charles Sousa, a seminary junior, for help and, having a car, he agreed to fill in.

Chuck set out at 6:30 a. m., determined to be punctual, but his car broke down fifteen miles north of Bangor. The temperature beside the Penobscot River was below zero, and no telephone was anywhere near. What to do? He locked his car and hoisted his thumb. Almost at once he was picked up by an immigration officer bound for the Canadian border. The officer questioned his rider closely and, after he was treated to a preview of the young minister's Sunday morning message, he decided his passenger was indeed a preacher.

Sousa arrived at his first service in Hodgdon just on time, but reached the second, one minute late. He fell in behind the choir proceeding toward the front of the church. A deacon thrust a bit of notepaper with the hymn numbers into his hand, and the young parson marched to the pulpit.

His return to Bangor also was accomplished by the effective use of his thumb. After a snack and a nap he and a classmate, who knows about engines, retrieved his disabled car. If I asked Chuck to go to Fort Kent next Sunday, he'd grin and start out.

February 12

I seldom discover either student pastors or full-time ministers so attached to their present parishes that they would be unwilling to "advance" to a larger church which could offer a more generous salary, a more commodious parsonage, and a more fully equipped church plant. Occasionally though, I do find a minister staying in the same community all the time he is in Seminary and then remaining several years after graduation and ordination.

This afternoon I relished a visit from an alumnus who has been in his present Aroostook parish eight years: three years as a student and five years as a full-time minister after graduation. A very personable and warm human being, he could have been enthusiastically accepted as minister by some thriving city church. Many ministers would have served two, even three, churches while he has been pleased to serve one.

We are old friends so I dared to ask, "Bob, how does it happen you've stayed put so long? I know you could be right now the minister of a much larger church. Why have you been content to stay eight years in an out-of-the-way community, living in a rambling parsonage, and existing on a modest salary?"

He told me he plans to stay even longer, "When I look at the same faces in the congregation each Sunday and often during the week, too, I never fail to find something new in them. It's really more exciting

to stay than to travel up from church to church trying to get to the top."

It's plain that he thinks he's arrived at the top already. As he left my office, he added this: "Really
I'm serving the ideal church. I know it's not a large
one, but the people are great workers, and that means
a lot to me. The custodian manages the building;
the music committee manages the choir; the deacons
manage the benevolences; and the trustees manage the
finances. All I have to do is manage myself!"

Maybe he *has* arrived at the top.

February 16

It seems as though, down in Hancock County,
there's a Sullivan for every point of the compass.
(On reflecting I can't remember a *South* Sullivan.)
Recently I accepted an invitation to attend a meeting
of the trustee board of one of the Sullivan churches.

The student minister wasn't present and frankness
was rampant about his performance, or lack of it.
To my astonishment, after he had been thoroughly
taken apart by several rather loud critics, he was voted
a salary raise.

On the evening's agenda was an item about the minister's non-care of the parsonage and grounds. This
item provoked a red-hot give-and-take among all board
members, some of whom got really abrasive. Some
members defended the pastor's upkeep of the manse;
others declared with vigor that he should be a more
competent caretaker. Among the people present,
three were especially articulate:

Trustee One "The water keeps freezing in the cellar

81

pipes; the reverend should not bank the house so carelessly; the reverend should keep the yard cleaner in summer and mow the lawn oftener; the reverend should get on the double windows in October rather than put off the business until the last of November."

Trustee Two "Keeping the place looking respectable is O.K. but for my money the big deal is those water pipes. They shouldn't be allowed to freeze up every time we get a cold snap. This student's almost as dumb as the pastor we had who plugged the drain by flushing spuds down the john."

Trustee Three "I've been hearing a lot of beefing all around town about the parson's carelessness in protecting those water pipes. Well, the freeze-ups are not all his fault; it's our job in the first place to provide a decent house for him to live in. Last week when I knew the minister was attending classes at the Seminary I did some snooping at the parsonage. I walked around the house about four times. I can't say we ought to blame the preacher too much for frozen pipes. I counted ten holes in the cellar wall you could throw a cat through."

After a moment of silence the chairperson of the board called attention to the next item on the agenda.

February 18

"The preacher we've got here now is a pretty crude guy, a real odd fish. He didn't succeed in business and he's sure a bust as a minister. Just to show you how atrocious his manners are, he keeps his lower teeth in a glass of water under the pulpit instead of in his mouth where they ought to be. Awful!"

All this came from a male member of a church in Franklin County. There is some truth in what he said I guess. At any rate, truth or not, I was compelled out of politeness to listen to more, much more, as we stood on the church steps. The deacon bellowed so I felt that all the good people up and down the road would become alarmed. I was tempted to suggest that we withdraw to behind the church where his trumpet tones would be muffled somewhat.

The dubious opinion aired by the deacon was not echoed by all church members. Others in the congregation were far less severe with their parson who is indeed rough-hewn. They spoke of his winsomeness with little children who love him warmly. A carpenter of sorts, he has helped mend a neighbor's roof, propped up a pulp-cutter's leaning woodshed, attached a creditable stoop to a trailer. All these services, and many more he has rendered without thought of bribing the recipients into attending worship!

The biggest compliment to the minister came from a female citizen who did not think she was commending him at all. Said she: "He spends too much time with the down-and-outers and riff-raff; he attracts to church meetings the drunks and bums who'd never be welcome in any of those fancy Farmington churches."

February 20

A committee from the Newport Congregational

Church visited the Seminary today in search of a student pastor. The members of the group met with me and four students who are interested in standing as candidates for the position. After introducing the students to the committee I encouraged the visitors to describe their church, its special needs, and the kind of service they expect from a minister. Also, I invited the candidates to express to the committee their feelings about their role as student pastors.

Inwardly I was diverted by the forthright statements made by all four students, each of whom wanted to be chosen to serve this parish that so long has relied upon the Seminary for leadership. It did not seem to occur to any of them that they were tripping over their tongues and perhaps damaging their chances of success.

First Student: "The church I'm looking for is one where the members promise to work just as hard at being Christians as they expect the minister to. I don't plan to be the only hard worker in the church."

Second Student: "Please don't expect me to shave my beard and be dressed up all the time; I hate neckties.

Third Student: "If you should ask me to become your pastor I think it only fair you should know that my family comes first with me, then my studies, and the church last."

Fourth Student: " Maybe some Sundays I won't be able to preach a sermon because I haven't thought up anything to say. If that should happen I'd have to call off the service."

At first the committee did not take kindly to this

last warning, though one member did say thoughtfully in a kind of an aside, "It would be better to refuse to preach if you've nothing to say than to go ahead and preach with nothing to say." The aside was caught up by other members, and behold, the student's honesty and bluntness contributed to his being chosen as the Newport pastor. I wonder whether some Sunday I'll get a phone call from a distressed member of the church asking for a substitute preacher for the morning service: "Our minister just doesn't have a thing to say to us today."

February 21

The morning's mail brought this bit of spice:
Dear Reverend Cook:

This minister you sent us is totally impractical. Do you know what he wants us to do? He wants us to keep the church unlocked every day. This little church! He says it's so people can go in and have private worship in the middle of the week. It wouldn't be so bad in summer; after all there's nothing that anyone would steal, except perhaps the offering plates which were given to us by a couple of visitors last summer.

But in February! Think of the fuel bill! We've never done any such thing before and I don't think we should start now. What do you think? A boy in the youth fellowship is the only one I've ever seen in there in the middle of the week meditating, and I don't see why he can't meditate just as well at home.

And another thing. I get sick and tired hearing this student of yours talk about 'Maine weather.' Last Friday when the blizzard hit us I knew we'd hear about the weather, and sure enough, during announcements on Sunday, he had to make a crack about how much tougher the weather here is than in Pennsylvania. What I would like to ask him is, if Maine's such a terrible place why doesn't he go to some school in Florida or Texas where everything's always so heavenly? And he's all the time lambasting 'Maine characters,' 'Maine drivers,' the 'Maine accent,' and what he calls the 'Maine state of mind.'

And that isn't all . . .

The letter writer's second point wins my sympathy. "Lambasting" Maine touches a sensitive nerve with me. I've been here myself well over fifty-five years and wouldn't live anywhere else. And besides, the student who now finds Maine offensive in so many ways may someday be delighted, upon his graduation, to accept an invitation to become a full-time parson in one of our churches.

February 23

Gathering examples of boners by beginners in all professions can be a diverting pastime. People beginning in the ministry do contribute their share.

Boner 1

A student supply spoke at the Cherryfield Congregational Church. He arrived well before service time to become familiar with the order of worship, which he studied with the organist. After a moment's thought while chewing the end of a pencil he crossed out the *Gloria Patri*. The organist inquired, "Aren't you including the Gloria in the service? We always sing it."

"I left it out," said the straightforward lad, "because I thought probably nobody down here in the sticks could play it."

Boner 2

Richard Norsworthy, the student minister at the Dexter Universalist Church, has been much troubled that the back pews during worship are well filled, but the front ones are empty; so, he roped off the last four on either side of the center aisle. At announcement time he told the congregation that the roped-off seats were for a very special group of people. "When I make pastoral calls," he declared, "I hear many of our church members say, 'We don't get around to church much on Sundays, but we want you to know we're with you in spirit.' The roped-off back pews are for those who are with us in spirit. It's a pity they can't put anything in the offering."

Boner 3

A young hothead is serving the Methodist Church at Bar Harbor. He has a tiny study in the church building where he prepares his sermons. The study is a kind of converted storeroom where have been kept church school supplies, a mimeographing machine, candelabra, and wornout Bibles. The people of the church haven't been able to get out of the habit of barging into the study to find crayons, dust cloths, and rubber bands. The pastor, having grown indignant over such intrusions, finally placed a sign on the "office" door which read: KEEP OUT

OF THE ROOM. THIS INCLUDES CHURCH OFFICERS.

Boner 4

The student minister at the Mattawamkeag Methodist Church has been especially short on tact. On a recent Sunday a member of the church now living in Waterville returned to Mattawamkeag for a visit and attended worship. After being introduced to her at the close of the service the student inquired, "Why don't you get a letter of transfer from here and join the Waterville Methodist Church since you're living there?" The lady replied that she might not continue to live there. "Well," said the student, "the way it is now you're not doing any good here, and you're not doing any good there; you ought to plan on doing some good somewhere."

Boner 5

Too often student ministers, lacking in knowledge of parliamentary law, foul up the orderliness of church business meetings.

A young junior in his first year as student pastor of a small church in Somerset County had a rough time at the annual meeting. A moot question was before the members of the church; leading voices on both sides were agitated and loud, but finally there came a motion and a second — followed by more dispute. After a few minutes of this, the young parson had a suggestion, "Why not just take Mrs. Brown's movement and lay it on the table?"

February 26

Rummaging around in one of the Seminary's old

storerooms I came across a story about Professor Ralph Adams who years ago was field service director here.

It seems he visited a small church in Hancock County where a student was serving only half-heartedly. The congregation expressed its dissatisfaction to Adams who next day summoned the student to his office for a "consultation."

The student was prepossessing, although a trifle on the languid side. He readily confessed his negligence in church work. Adams decided to stiff-arm him, hoping to arouse his determination to give more of himself. The student remained good-humored and non-defensive while Adams banged him about.

"Let's see," asked Adams, "how many members in the church you serve?"

"Twenty-two."

"And how many are really committed members?"

"All twenty-two."

This stopped Adams, because he had been informed by a church member that congregations were dwindling and offerings were falling off. So Adams pressed in.

"Twenty-two members, and twenty-two are committed. Now look here, that's not the picture I'm getting from some of the congregation. You really mean to say that all twenty-two are dedicated?"

"Sure," said the student, "all of them, eleven dedicated to keeping me, eleven dedicated to getting rid of me."

March 1

The young fellow who serves the Island Falls Congregational Church was too ill to preach yesterday; so, at the last minute I filled in for him.

What a hospitable fellowship! The cordial welcome I received included a cup of steaming coffee, a talk with a fellow angler who for five minutes swapped trout-fishing stories with me, and an organ prelude that warmed my soul.

After a few pleasant exchanges with the head usher I sat down behind the pulpit waiting for the service to begin and observed the astonishing performance of a well-dressed woman in a tomato-colored hat, white gloves, and heels. Just before eleven o'clock, service time, she rose from a pew, went to the rear of the sanctuary, and tugged at a bell rope, spending a good long three minutes in vigorous exercise. About forty-five worshipers occupied pews, among them were at least a dozen stalwart men. The lady completed her assignment, adjusted a somewhat tilted hat and resumed her seat beside a husky potato farmer, presumably her husband.

I got so absorbed in this drama that I gave a tardy call to worship.

Driving home from the Falls church I thought of a possible area for research: discover *why* sextons of almost all churches ring the belfry bell during or after the prelude. I understand the value of a warning bell a half hour before the service, but ringing the bell at the start of the service is a hopeless business. It's far too late then to rout delinquents out of bed in time for the service.

Footnote: At least half a dozen churches I've visited during the last year have bell towers that are apparently too large for the rest of the building. Just last week I sat in a church where the ringing of the bell made the whole structure vibrate nervously as though we were jarred slightly by a distant quake. A church steeple, no matter how esthetically appealing, is a great waste of material anyhow; it's a pity, and a little alarming, that some of these towers sustain bells that, when rung on Sunday mornings, shake the entire building.

March 8

Monday mornings strange tales filter into the field education office about the weekend adventures of the several dozen student pastors and substitute preachers who have fanned out to churches all over Maine. I believe, from what the Danville Junction student pastor told me this morning about his experience yesterday, that he must be one of the most resourceful of all church workers.

Early in the morning he set off for the Danville Church in his battered car. (Seeing it around the campus I have often wondered how it holds together to carry the preacher over two hundred miles round trip each weekend.) About twelve miles along Interstate 95 a tire blew. He quickly replaced it with a very smooth article that surely had only a few miles left in it.

The tire held, surprising the family of six packed into the car. But about twenty miles farther along, the fan belt broke. The student got out and lifted the hood to discover the belt was not only broken but missing. After searching under the car seats, and rummaging through his trunk for a replacement, and finding none, he pulled off his trousers belt and used it to connect the water pump and drive shaft pulley. After this time-consuming operation he was on his way again, and managed to roll into the Junction just in time to announce the opening hymn.

Following the account of his weekend experience, reported quite matter-of-factly, he left the office for a Monday class. Suddenly I realized he had not told me what held up his pants while he preached his sermon.

March 11

A student on his way from Bangor to supply a pulpit near Rumford drove by the Skowhegan Roman Catholic Church. Cars of Catholic worshipers lined both sides of the street for a quarter mile. The student growled to himself, "What's wrong with Protestant churches? Only a dozen or two cars in front of them."

An hour and a half later he arrived at the church where he was to preach, with the picture of the overflowing Roman Catholic church still fresh in his mind. During his sermon at a sparsely attended service he asked the rhetorical question: "What's wrong with Protestant churches, anyhow?" Far back in the congregation a worshiper's hand shot up. The preacher continued, and again wove the question into his sermon, and again the worshiper's hand waved high in the air. The third time the student fired the question and saw the hand vigorously waving, he got the idea the worshiper really did want to say something. The student broke off his sermon and invited the man to speak up. The man rose and shouted, "I'll tell you what's wrong with Protestant churches; it's you preachers," and sat down.

The daring student, apparently capable of absorbing much punishment, tried unsuccessfully, at the close of the service, to find the hand-waving protester to learn more. My guess is, if the man *had* been found, the student would have gotten his ego soundly thumped.

March 14

The general impression that women are the backbone of churches was surely confirmed at the service this morning in a Washington County church where I sat in a pew to observe a student minister conduct worship. Thirty-five ladies were in the sanctuary; there were two men: the student and I.

When the time came during the service for passing the offering plate, I found that ladies still shrink from some tasks in service to the church. After the student announced the offering, nothing happened except that the organist rendered a voluntary. There was much craning of necks on the part of the all-lady congregation to see who would serve as an usher. For what seemed to me a full five minutes the service remained at dead center. I was tempted to offer my assistance, but because I was only a visitor I sat tight.

At last a woman in a back pew rose and went out the rear door of the church. She reappeared with a tousle-haired red-faced teenage boy who gathered the contributions. He left the plate, looking like a tossed salad (the ladies were very generous), on a shelf at the rear of the room, and disappeared.

Why, I wondered, are women, so often the budget directors at home, so shy of passing the plate in church? Certainly offering plates are never heavy enough to cause even the frailest female to falter under their weight. Half of the Maine churches are served by women treasurers, but still they are put to rout at the thought of performing the collecting act.

March 22

Ralph Cook, considered quite suave and self-confident by his professors and peers, has just been elected student minister at the East Bangor Congregational Church. His usual urbanity hardly survived several harrowing incidents yesterday while he attempted to conduct worship in the vestry of the church.

A mother, apparently a most permissive parent, attended worship with her three small and restless children. During the sermon one little girl deserted the mother, and wandered up the aisle to the front pew which she "filled" for the remainder of the service. She sprawled, stretched, dropped hymnbooks, yawned noisily, hiccupped, slid back and forth on the pew, turned about to stare into the faces of other worshipers, and wave blithely to her brother and sister three seats back. The child's restlessness must have been contagious because several other children whispered and squirmed.

Ralph told me that he was really upset. He

94

stopped preaching and sought to induce a more reverent spirit of worship by bowing in prayer — although he had already prayed three times in the service. After he said, "Let us pray," the child in the front pew called out loudly, "What, again?" The congregation was much amused (anything's funny in church), but the struggling pastor was not pleased at all.

In the same service Ralph had a lively skirmish with a huge fly that, far ahead of warm spring days, wheeled and buzzed around his head and belted window panes during the offering, anthem, and sermon.

Such static even seasoned ministers find hard to take in stride. Ralph, his composure shattered, decided not to complete his sermon; he announced the closing hymn: "Number 146 — 'How Sweet and Silent Is the Place'."

March 23

From Seminary Hill to Tenants Harbor is a fairly long drive — longer in March than in June, or so it seems. To be sure that I would arrive in time this past Sunday morning I set out early for the Harbor, even though bare roads and a touch of spring assured me of safe driving. Dodging March potholes and taking frost heaves with caution I drove into town well before service time at the Baptist church — a venerable old building — where I was to preach.

The service started at 10:30 and having a full half hour before getting behind the pulpit, I stopped at a lunch counter for a doughnut and coffee.

A stout waitress served me, and seeming to want a conversation, asked who I was. After my reply that I was from Bangor Seminary and was filling in one Sunday as a preacher at the Baptist Church, she slumped down on a stool near the candy counter and reported at length on the rough way "that church" has handled previous ministers.

The last minister, she told me, arrived in a snow-storm. Three trustees cleared his drive to the parson-age so he could move in his wife, children, and furni-ture. She continued that when the town "character" observed the busy shovelers, he commented, "They're shoveling in the new preacher; in three months they'll be shoveling him the hell out again."

Some churches are known as being hard on minis-ters. I usually find them no harder on ministers than ministers are hard on *them*.

Occasionally a student pastor gets "shoveled to hell out" because he no sooner moves into the parsonage than he is gung ho for changing everything he finds in the church, from the constitution and by-laws to the color of the choir's gowns. Hardly has his wife hung curtains in their new home than he's off on a program of reform.

There is little use in warning him against trying to revolutionize the whole structure of the church in one month; he's certain he'll need but one week. The present church school material is asinine, he an-nounces, and must be replaced — at once. The com-munion table, he goes on, is in the wrong position and must be "altared" — now. The hymn books

are passe and should be given to the Salvation Army —
before another Sunday.

Student ministers usually survive the vexation of
church members who object to the young preachers
trying to transform overnight the church organization, parish house, and order of worship. People in
the pews do get a bit jumpy about bellicose sermons
in which some pastors set about eliminating at one
clip all of the injustices and inequities in U. S. society. Church people have often said this: "If our pastor
will just get to know us and trust us, and will help us
to work on one project at a time, we'll cooperate."

At any rate, few preachers get "shoveled out."

March 24

The visits I made today on members of a church
near Machias made my head spin. Their student
minister has been working with them a year and a
half. As usual I asked questions about his effectiveness. From the first two people I interviewed I got
the following contradictory evaluations. (Can they
be talking about the same guy?)

The Church Organist: "He's a great disappoint-
ment. We had hoped for a student who would preach
sermons we'd enjoy, but we go home to dinner every
Sunday drooping. He's always butting into my business of playing the organ, asking me to play this and
play that for preludes and offertories. He's constant-
ly experimenting with the order of worship and showing off all the knowledge he's getting from you Seminary teachers. He's ready at the drop of a hymn book
to make the congregation sing some tune we've never

heard before and can't sing when we try. The next time you send a minister down here from that school I hope you'll remember that we're a quiet little community and don't want to be all stirred up by a little whippersnapper of a beginning preacher who thinks he's real smart but really has so much to learn he's pitiful."

Whew!

The Church School Superintendent: "He's all we could have hoped for in a student minister. His sermons may not always send us out with stars in our eyes but they are solid and sensible and always have some encouraging words in them. Thank goodness he takes an interest in the church school and makes helpful suggestions about classroom rearrangements and about lesson books. He seems to be learning all the time, and we are all the while profiting from the information he is getting in his courses at the Seminary — especially from those taught by your professor of Christian education. He has a whole basketful of ideas and every now and then persuades us to try one. Those we've tried have worked, too. We needed a minister to wake us up; this fellow's just right for us."

How about that!

March 26

"What *is* ecumenicity anyhow?" A layman from the Frankfort Congregational Church asked the question. Standing on the steps of the Seminary chapel, after a lay school lecture on theology, he looked really puzzled. "I have trouble just trying to pronounce the word," he said, "but I guess it means something like cooperation among denominations, doesn't it?"

I asked the layman whether he would attend an ecumenical Lenten service with me on the following Wednesday evening, hoping he might pick up a few clues about the meaning of the word that was mystifying him so. He did accompany me and came away from the service saying he was getting a hint of the meaning of ecumenicity. "At least," he remarked, "I believe I've learned how to pronounce it."

Present at the service were Baptists, Roman Catholics, Lutherans, Congregationalists, Methodists, and Presbyterians — all worshiping together. A Methodist student minister gave the call to worship, a Baptist pastor read the Scripture, a Roman Catholic priest preached the sermon, and a Congregationalist student minister offered a pastoral prayer and pronounced the benediction.

Twenty-five years ago such an event would have been impossible even to imagine. A deacon from the All Souls Church in Bangor commented after the service: "Every year when Lent comes around we take this ecumenical thing for granted." One of the student pastors, overwhelmed by all the visible fellowship, affirmed that the service had been as important to him as his own conversion experience. During the fellowship hour at the close of the meeting the same student observed that "all these good Christians look alike to me, I can't tell the difference between Roman Catholics and Protestants."

The many differences among these denominations are by no means obliterated, or even reconciled, but the evening of ecumenical worship was unmistakably significant to all.

March 27

Here we go again! One of my colleagues on the faculty is taking a clutch of students and student ministers to an out-of-state "radical" conference. The fire-eating conference speakers will enlarge on how all denominations are dismantling the true faith and becoming simply reflections of our decadent culture. Some students will return with a full head of steam to alter, reform, cleanse, or even smash the present structures of the churches they serve.

Certainly the reform impulse is needed in many a student-served church; but the raw and headlong approach some fledgling student ministers may adopt after returning from the conference will confuse and divide a mystified congregation.

"Hey," some bewildered church member will protest, "what's got into the minister? During Sunday service he raked us over the coals because he said we're not out saving the world. He's just got back from some conference, and is he ever loaded for bear! If he'd held a talk-back after the service, we sure would have told him something for his own good."

The latest howl just came from a deacon of a Piscataquis County church whose minister recently returned from an "inspiring" conference in Massachusetts. His pastor is a young man of twenty-five, dedicated, sincere, capable, enthusiastic — and so impetuous!

The deacon reported that the student dramatically discarded the gown he has been wearing while conducting public worship and told the congregation he was never again going to wear it in the pulpit. Also, the deacon continued, the minister invited the choir members, if they really wanted to serve the Lord, to throw aside their gowns, too. The congregation is now completely at sea, because during the weeks prior to this explosion the student not only wore a pulpit gown but also different colored stoles, the liturgical significance of which he carefully explained to the congregation.

The following Sunday not only was the minister ungowned, but the organist too, who, in a green turtle-neck sweater, sat at the elevated organ console. "How come?" bewildered worshipers wanted to know, and then loudly complained to the pastor.

The young minister lamely tried to explain — after the furor reached its peak — that he was emphasizing how the gap between pulpit and pew should be closed. "We are *all* ministers of the Lord," he declared, "and I'm no different from you. Every one of you religious people ought to be out working for God. That gown of mine stresses that I'm set apart, and I want no more of it."

Of course the student is correct about the significant part the lay people should play in church endeavors. If only the young man's "radicalism" — that is what his critics called it — could be controlled and his spirit tempered, he might lead the people he serves to a new vision of their own equal role in the church instead of making them mad.

April 2

Paul Paskewitz, the young man who thumbed to Limington, is now eligible to serve as pastor of a church. He has been at Seminary over a year and has shown that he can do passing work in the classroom. Paul has had an indistinct image of himself. He has hoped he might be worthy of an opportunity to become pastor of a church but has doubted whether he could preach acceptably, or lead a congregation in any way. In fact he has been so unsure of himself that, although he wanted to serve God in a church, his self doubts have held him back from candidating for a church.

Three weeks ago, overcoming a little of his dubious estimate of himself, he preached a "trial" sermon in the Congregational Church in Weld, then waited nervously — and gloomily — to hear whether the church would accept him. He was certain that his candidating sermon sounded like so much nonsense.

At last, word came to my office from Dorothy Winter, clerk of the Weld church, that Paskewitz was wanted. Although at first he was overcome with joy, his ecstatic feelings were short lived. After his initial jubilation he did some thinking and told me: "I don't know about all this; I'm not sure I want to be pastor of a church that is willing to take me."

April 5

"Yesterday I gave 'em my resignation."

The words were mumbled to me by a short-haired, red-faced junior as we climbed the stairs to my office. He said that the day before he had "blown his cork" and quit the church he had been serving. I stopped on the top stair and looked at him. There he stood facing me, a little ashamed, a little bewildered, not sure the morning-after why he had sounded off and charged the startled people in the pews with apathy, laziness, laxity, and a host of other short-comings. He hadn't *tendered* his resignation; in a fit of pique he had *fired* it at the congregation. And they had accepted it. Now, less than twenty-four hours later he wasn't sure any more about what he had done, or about himself, or about his future.

After his explosion some of the people in his parish were uneasy over his eruption; others were nettled; still others were relieved. Some members of the group admitted to apathy and laxity, but felt the young fellow had "shot from the hip."

Despite his Sunday assault on the congregation, I do feel the boy has promise. Perhaps next time, if he graduates and serves another church, he'll have learned, when angry and frustrated, to burst forth in the ear of a sympathetic friend, not in the face of a congregation.

Sometimes a student hard-pressed academically, falling behind in his studies because he is devoting too much time to church work, will come to feel he must read his resignation. Now and then, a student whose parish is a hundred miles and more from School will, after a year of service, decide he must resign to keep his family together. "My wife," he may say, "gets terribly lonely in the parsonage while I am at school four days a week."

But "I gave 'em my resignation yesterday," can

mean that the student has had a fight with some cantankerous deacon, or has grown resentful of well-meant criticism from a church officer, or has lapsed into chronic irritability because he has failed to reform the whole town in six long months. Now and then a beginning preacher will drum away incessantly on a single preaching note — pacifism, sexism, death, racial justice — until listeners know just what to expect every Sunday from the pulpit. His congregation gets bored, then hostile, and finally outspokenly sore. Then comes an explosion from a vexed member, a counter explosion from the preacher, followed by "I resign . . .!"

Another kind of "resignation" took place years ago at the East Bangor Congregational Church on the Pushau Road. The student serving the church apparently was never officially "called" to be the minister, but simply filled in Sunday to Sunday until everybody took it for granted he was the regularly hired pastor. One Sunday he did not appear to lead worship. Investigation revealed he had quit school all of a sudden and left town. Later I asked the church clerk whether the student had ever sent in his resignation.

"Huh," she sniffed, "how could he resign: We never hired him."

April 10

The clerk of a small church parish in Somerset County is a writer of wistful letters that always tug at my sympathy. This morning one arrived which asked, "Do you think that soon you may be able to send us somebody from the Seminary who can serve as our regular student minister?"

For months, since the last student resigned to accept an appointment to a larger parish, I have been sending supply preachers to this church — a different one each Sunday. So far I have not found one student available to work with the church regularly on weekends.

The good people of this church have converted an abandoned schoolhouse into a parsonage where a student may stay on Saturdays and Sundays; they have done all their few dollars can do to improve the church property; they are willing to pay until it hurts for student help. But up to now a Sunday sermon by a different student each weekend is all I have been able to provide for them.

Many other churches cannot understand why I do not send them several candidates. It is taken for granted that on a *student* level at least, the Seminary should have a locker full of applicants. "Why is it," I am asked, "that with over one hundred students in your school you cannot send us a half dozen to choose from?"

One reason why student ministers are in short supply was suggested by the chairperson of the executive committee of a small Aroostook County Congregational church. At a recent meeting of the committee, all members were wondering out loud why "student parsons" were scarce. Finally the chairperson exploded: "Well, ministers have to come from *somewhere*. How about us? How many young men and women have we sent into the ministry from this church? I've been a member here over forty years and I can't recollect a single one!"

April 14

"I enjoyed your sermon."

This is the most common expression of peoples' appreciation of student ministers' presentations as they shake his hand at the close of morning worship. Often students, among themselves, speak slightingly of this compliment, referring to it as "just a stock phrase," a polite remark worshipers feel they must make when they go out the church door.

It is wrong to belittle the comment, I remind students. Though often the expression may seem meaningless, it may be the worshipers' way of saying, "Your sermon gave me a bit of light on a dark day."

Of course, student ministers need to learn that a healthy humility will forbid them absorbing all the lavish applause they may get for their preaching. One student commented to me after a parishioner had praised his sermon profusely: "It was like perfume, I sniffed it, but I didn't swallow it." But time and again I have seen beginning student pastors prone to believe everything they are told — especially if they are complimented.

About a year ago, student Hugh Reed became the minister of the Ellsworth Falls Congregational Church. The first few Sundays he preached fifteen-minute sermons his hearers said were helpful. After six months he preached half-hour sermons people didn't like at all. I checked with Reed to find out why he had doubled the length of his sermons. It seems that during the first few months of his work people going out of the church door after the service commended him for helpful messages. Several said: "That was a good sermon, pastor, we enjoyed it, we could have listened twice as long." Reed innocently took the words seriously and literally. After a while, increasing sophistication will persuade him to take all compliments more guardedly.

Sometimes worshipers' comments on sermons are highly cryptic. Students who have listened to them have frequently quoted to me some of the mysterious remarks that worshipers have made when going out the church door at the close of services. I cannot give the vaguest interpretation of the following after-sermon observations:

"Well, you sure pushed the throttle to the floor this morning."

"That was quite a brew you steeped for us today."

"That sermon made me think of my aunt's washing machine."

"After your sermon I felt like a jilted buzzard."

"I kind of liked that sermon; it tantalized me."

Regrettably there's little chance to follow up these perplexing statements which cry aloud for explanation. By the time the minister has recovered from the shock of one, the worshiper who fired the shot has driven off in his car and headed for Sunday dinner.

(No member of the Seminary community has a more distinguished and venerable presence than the Old Testament professor of language and literature, Dr. Stephen Szikszai. For over twenty-two years he has held the post. Often he has filled Maine pulpits as a substitute preacher. Recently a thirteen-year-old girl shook his hand after the morning service and commended him for a helpful sermon. Said she: "That was really groovy, keep up the good work, feller.")

April 16

About two months ago student Norman Dubie, a Seminary junior, a husky, impressive-looking fellow, stood as a candidate for the Phippsburg Church. Before going there to preach his trial sermon, much discussion in his home centered upon this coming event. Dubie and his wife frequently shared their hopes, apprehensions, and strategy. Their two young sons, Norman Jr. and Robert, listened intently and became involved. The topic came alive about every day in the home.

"Dad," Norman asked one evening, "does your getting that church depend upon how good you preach?"

"If I fail in the pulpit, I don't get it," his dad said. "It's as simple as that."

Little Norman pondered a while, then said, "I think you'd better preach one of those sermons from the Peter Marshall book." He did, and got the invitation to serve the church.

Dubie's misgivings are typical of students preaching their first sermon, especially when a call to become pastor of a church depends upon the effectiveness of their preaching. They worry and fret and stew. They pace the floor early on the Sunday morning they are candidating, speak abruptly to their children, can't eat their breakfasts, and are anxious whether the car will start (sometimes they go out to start it two or three times before it is time to leave for church). They moan about their lack of holiness for the hallowed task before them. They may say something like, "I'm just not good enough to lead people in worship; who am I to preach to people who have been church members longer than I've been living?"

One student's wife, a little oppressed by her husband's breast beating, exclaimed: "Now dear, just remember you're up in that pulpit to talk about God, not *be* God."

April 17

Today, student Robert Mitchell walked over to the library with me after a church history lecture. Bob takes a lively interest in the Christian education work of his parish; he told me of his dismay that so many "of my kids are always late for church school classes."

He is an ingenious sort of a fellow so I imagined he was already planning some strategy that would correct his young folk's habits of tardiness.

"What are you going to do about such slackness?" I wanted to know.

"Well," he said, "I suppose the Old and New Testament departments of Bangor Seminary would not approve, but next month instead of awarding Revised Standard Versions of the Bible to the youngsters graduating into the high school department, I'm switching to alarm clocks."

April 19

This morning a letter came from a ladies' aide

president in Washington County. I got a real pang as I read it; small wonder that an up-and-coming student with a sense of mission gets discouraged.

Dear Sir:

Now Dr. Cook, we have a nice little church here. It's just right the way it is, and we want to keep it this way. But this student we've got for a minister wants to "improve" everything.

He says the Sunday school classes shouldn't be meeting in the same place where we have our morning service. So he wants to turn our pretty balcony into classrooms. Our weather vane is tilted a little bit to one side from one of the Northeasters we got last winter, and he says that's a disgrace with the church standing close to the road as it does. So he wants to have it straightened right now, and while we're at it paint the whole church.

We told him — our Ladies' Aide told him — the church was painted just twelve years ago and it could wait another five for that. He wants to knock the back pews out of the church to make room for bookcases for a library. And he wants a wooden walk built from the road way to the front door of the church.

He's a good little minister and puts up a real nice sermon and he sees the sick people, but he wants us to do too much. And now he's found out we've got a little money in our Ladies' Aide bank account (our treasurer made a mistake and told him), he'll push harder than ever to "make improvements," as he calls them.

Will you talk with him Dr. Cook, and tell him we want things to stay as they are. As I said, we've got a nice little church and we don't think anything much needs changing. Most of us are

110

old ladies and we're lame, but we like to work for our church the best we can.

Yours truly,
The president

After reading the letter I decided to go visiting, not only in the village from which the letter came, but in several other hamlets near it where we have placed student ministers.

When down in the Jonesport-Meddybemps-Eastport country I always try to see Keith Kilby who has lived in Maine all his life and runs a grocery store near the Dennysville River. Kilby is an amiable personality whose salty remarks show uncanny understanding of the way many Down Easters think.

As usual I found him in his store. No customers were present — not even the usual loafer who sits on the soft drink cooler. In our conversation I mentioned to him the complaint of the ladies' aide president who feels her student minister is too progressive. Of course, I did not identify the lady nor the village where she lives.

As I expected, Keith was ready with a pungent commentary on the church members he knows so well in his own town of Dennysville. "People down this way all want a dignified, quiet sort of minister to talk kindly to 'em on Sundays, comfort 'em when they're sick, and let 'em alone the rest of the time. No parson who really wants to do things oughta come down here. These folks are old fashioned when it comes to preachers. They want up-to-date cars but they want a Model-T minister."

April 20

A pulpit committee from a church near Moosehead Lake met with me in the Seminary faculty room at 7 p.m. I was impressed by their punctuality: Moosehead is a long way from Bangor; yet, everyone was on time, and they came in different cars. Sometimes committee members from nearby villages show up half an hour late.

A lady member of the committee displayed a scrapbook with pasted-in newspaper pictures of several previous ministers of her church. "Don't you think we deserve a *good*-looking one this time?" she asked me. "Some of these preachers we've had have been saintly enough alright, but just look at them! This time we'd like to get one for our pulpit who doesn't remind us of pictures of men I notice in the Post Office with numbers across their chests. After all, we have to sit and look at them for a whole hour every Sunday."

Similar requests have been expressed before, although audio-visual aids, such as this scrapbook, have not been employed to convince me of a congregation's yearning for a more photogenic minister. Occasionally, when churches write to me to send them a candidate for their vacant pulpit, they request a picture before they agree to hear the person. (In some cases, when the prospective candidate is a man, I am tempted to send his wife's picture.)

Last week in Somerset County I met with members of a pulpit committee in search of a new minister. As we settled around the table in the kitchen of the church I asked: "What especially do you hope for from your next student minister? Do you want him or her to emphasize work with youth, parish calling, church school supervision, or church administration?"

The committee confronted me with an unexpected requirement for a pastor. They were much concerned about the physical length and breadth of the next young parson. The depth of his commitment and the breadth of his knowledge of the Bible were, they admitted, surely important, but his body measurements were also important. I was puzzled for a while but finally the mystery was solved for me.

Six months before, the men's club of the church bought a flowing gown for the minister, with the understanding that when he resigned the church to serve another, he must leave the gown behind for the next minister, who in turn would pass it on to *his* successor. The pastor who had been serving the church, and lately wearing the gown, was a slender six feet two; the gown fitted him fine.

Candidates for this pastorate may have impressive intellectual and spiritual measurements, but if they are a chubby five feet three instead of a stringy six feet two, they won't get the invitation to serve. Fitting the gown is a prime requirement for fitting the job.

April 21

This afternoon I visited several members of one of the Methodist churches in Orrington. Patches of rotting snow and a couple of sagging snow fences reminded me, as I drove along the Penobscot and

113

through South Brewer toward the Orringtons, that this winter had hit us hard — as usual. No matter, today I *felt* spring. A strong wind and a few more warm days like this would see ice-out in most of the lakes I loved to fish.

But however I might dream about fishing, today I was on another kind of errand, I was in search of lay peoples' evaluation of their minister. First I called upon a talkative lady who must have seen me coming up the drive, for, by the time I had stepped into her kitchen, she had put out a cup of hot water and a tea bag. I did not need to announce to her that I was there to inquire about the church work being done by the student. She pitched a question to me before I could get comfortable in her kitchen rocking chair.

"Don't you have any courses at that Seminary for preachers' wives?" Right away from her tone I gathered she thought we needed several. She told me the student's wife was very rude. I half expected to hear that the lady of the parsonage interrupted her husband while he was preaching last Sunday's sermon, or insulted the most distinguished member of the church, or tongue-lashed the lay leader. Instead I learned that the offending wife "associates only with the younger women's group and often stays home when the older ladies' circle meets."

And why not? With two children in the parsonage and a busy husband to cook and wash and mend for, should she be expected to attend all meetings of all ladies' groups all of the time?

Despite this woman's protests, great changes are taking place in most churches' views of a pastor's

114

wife's responsibilities. No longer do many church members expect her to sing in the choir, teach a church school class, chair the missionary committee, and bake for every supper sponsored by the Bustling Busy Bees Sewing Circle.

Church members are also becoming less demanding of the student minister's wife. They are discovering for themselves that just because her husband is studying for the ministry, she is not necessarily a semi-minister herself. Sympathetic concern is growing for her, plus an increasing awareness of her loneliness, especially if her parsonage home is seventy-five miles or more from the Seminary where her husband is at school at least four days and three nights a week. If there are parsonage children, she must care for them with little or no help from him.

Although most church members expect less of a pastor's wife today, it is often the wife's skill in dealing with difficult and delicate situations that saves her husband from unpleasantness in parish service. A few years ago the Monson Community Church had a student minister, gifted and capable in many ways, but in human relations often thoughtless, brittle, and tart. In happy contrast, his wife was considerate, flexible, and tactful. More than once her winsomeness rescued him from his bruskness which threatened to impair friendly relations with church people.

April 22
One of the small Dixmont churches has been closed for years. It's a small, bare edifice, so dark that somehow it never seems to become much lighter no mat-

ter how many candles are set aglow on the Lord's table. Thank heaven the people are much warmer than their sanctuary. Recently, a handful of concerned people started a church school for about forty children. They asked over the telephone: "Now that we've got our Bible school going, we'd like to have some preaching, too. How much will it cost?"

"Well," I wanted to know, "how much can you raise?"

"Perhaps by 'taking around a paper' we can get a promise of five dollars a week."

While a couple of hopeful church members took around a paper, I set to work to find a student willing to drive to the church — thirty miles each way — for a five dollar bill every Sunday. The student would be expected to conduct worship, give guidance to church school, and make afternoon calls on the sick. The financial inducement was not exactly immense, but the first student I asked said, "Sure, I'll go down and see what I can do." He didn't even hesitate, and he thanked me for the opportunity.

Never will I be able to comprehend the economic innocence of some students. Again and again, students, shrewd enough in most ways, will entirely disregard the cost of gas, oil, and tires, and the wear and tear on their old cars. Given an opportunity to work in a church, off they blithely go.

Frequently I ask, "Do you think you can swing it? You have to eat, you know, and you have to buy new clothing once in a while." Back comes the usual, "If the Lord wants me in the ministry, he'll take care of me."

116

Sometimes I fling one more warning before I subside: "I commend you for your faith but you can't cash it at the supermarket." If that doesn't bring them up with a jolt, I quit arguing, just give them my blessing. And, oh my soul, I've seen it so often, the Lord does take care of such innocents.

On the contrary, many are far more practical and won't budge from the Seminary campus to serve a church until they are certain they "can do a little better than break even."

(I was treated today to an example of just how practical a few *church members* can be when they want a favor of the school. A lady member of a congregation forty miles from the campus wrote, "We need a speaker for our annual meeting. Do you have anyone at that Seminary who is Christian enough to come out and talk to us for nothing?" I resisted the impulse to write back at once: "Do you have any member of your church Christian enough to pay just the speaker's expenses?")

April 23

The Norridgewock Federated Church is living proof that Baptists and Congregationalists can worship God together under the same roof without fighting all the time. But for several weeks both denominations have had their parson under the gun. This evening I attended a meeting of church folk much put out with the obstinate young fellow who recently lost his head and "told 'em off" at announcement time during the morning service.

It's been hard for me to understand why this minister has been in such a really serious hassle with these good people. They've always been gracious and patient with all other ministers the Seminary has provided, even quick-tempered students.

This time the people were really wrathful; they wanted me to "get him out." I urged them to give him more time to prove himself, and after a lot of hostility was let loose the people simmered down and resolved to practice forbearance: "Well, maybe we *have* been a little rough on him. He does preach a pretty fair sermon."

One vigorous critic of the minister amused me — he had his own method of attacking the parson. Under the guise of asking questions he made speeches. I was reminded that this is a professorial technique — or disease — that often breaks out at student-faculty forums held in the Seminary conference rooms. Just because a sentence ends with a question mark is no sign at all that an interrogation is intended.

At any rate the critic did not influence the other church members to fire the pastor. He got a stay of execution. Now *I* must say a few things to *him*.

Maybe I'll ask him some questions.

April 24
Two students are serving in Searsport churches: Donald Dodds in the United Methodist; Richard Wyanski in the United Church of Christ. The church buildings are only a block apart. Although there is supposed to be no competition between these churches, only cooperation, some rivalry is inevitable. An

example of this rivalry comes into focus when a new Protestant family moves into town. Each pastor and each congregation will vie with the other to secure the favor and support of the new people.

Great credit is due both Dodds and Wyanski: each speaks highly of the other; they work together in a united youth group; they occasionally plan union services together; they share ideas.

Such cooperation and brotherly love was not always so apparent when another pair of Seminary students, years ago, served these churches. I guess I'll never forget how one of these men came to me to comment about his "opponent" in the other church. "He's terrific," said the student. "His sermons inspire, he's a topnotch pastor and never fails to call on the sick and shut-ins. He's a winner with the youth and a great planner of lively programs. His church officers think he's the greatest thing that ever hit Searsport; they'd go along with him if he took passenger space on a rocket to the moon. He has a winning personality to go with his good looks. He gives me a great big pain!"

April 26

Something I saw this morning was so wonderful!

On the bulletin board in Maine Hall was a "thank you" note. I read it twice and copied it down; it was so wonderful. Apparently, it was put up by a student who (anonymously) appreciates the forbearance and goodwill of the congregation he or she serves. It read as follows:

THANKS TO THE CONGREGATION

For saying you find help in the sermons I preach — even the ones I get up during final exam weeks at the Seminary;

For never asking that I operate as a triple wizard at preaching, praying, and leading the congregational singing;

For saying so many times you can see that I'm improving as pastor and preacher;

For bearing with me when I palm off my professors' lecture notes as fresh sermon material of my own;

For picking up responsibilities, in the parish, that I dropped;

For pretending not to notice how selfish I really am;

For not expecting me to actually carry out some of my silly proposals designed to double the Sunday attendance and triple the budget;

For overlooking my awkwardness the first time I baptized a baby and served communion;

For bearing with me when I stress the unimportant and slight the essential.

To see gratitude expressed this way is really amazing, although I'm certain that many students are grateful to the church people they serve. I do often hear them admit to one another that they could not feed their families if it were not for the help they received from their parishes.

Gratitude spelled out can be exceedingly pleasing. I know how pleased *I* was with two letters from former students. Two men wrote me to express appreciation for my making them available to churches. Their gratitude was the more pleasing because neither served parishes within easy traveling distance from the Seminary. Dick Arnold worked faithfully in the Springfield Congregational Church — seventy-five miles north of Bangor; Harry Flad gave his devotion to the Temple Federated Church — ninety miles west.

Surely a student who remembers with thanks the blessings of his first small parish will be too much occupied with those recollections to remember its faults.

April 27

Many churches have a weekly calendar that lists the order of service, announcements, news, and so forth. When the members of the worshiping community enter the sanctuary on Sundays about the first thing they do is pick up the calendar, which they read during the prelude. (When you come to think of it, a not very courteous activity while the organist is presumably faithfully rendering a musical selection.) Worshipers often choke over misprints that appear. Today, I added another boner to my collection.

Paul Whiting, a Seminary junior who serves the Deer Isle Congregational Church, advertised a hymn sing to be held in the vestry at the evening service this past Easter. The mimeographed calendar carried an invitation to all in the village to attend. Not yet expert in the operation of a typewriter (and probably in too great a hurry to proofread), Paul omitted a letter in just the wrong place. The notice

121

read: COME SIN WITH US TONIGHT. HOW
BETTER SPEND EASTER EVENING?

April 29

This morning I listened to a brace of sermons in
my homiletics class. Preaching sermons is an en-
grossing business, but trying to *teach* men and women
how to preach is a most improbable enterprise.

It's regrettable, but it does seem as though the
cocky, self-confident students are the more sought-
after preachers; they are the ones most often invited
to preach in large churches. The humble, self-ef-
facing minister doesn't "come on" impressively,
and often congregations in search of a preacher will
by-pass a loving, quiet-spoken, but capable candidate
for a "gee-whiz" guy who sounds as though he came
straight from Sinai with all the answers.

Today, a student not distinguished in the past
for humility came into preaching class shaking his
head, with modesty writ large in his manner. He
told me he was astonished how clearly and profound-
ly one of the deacons of the church he's serving in
Dover-Foxcroft thinks about Christianity.

Said the student, "That deacon knows the Bible
better than I do, and can explain a passage better,
too. He knows what he believes and is so convincing
about it that I learn more than I teach in the mid-week
Bible study I'm supposed to be leading. And think
of it," he added sorrowfully, "I'm taking six hours a
week of Old Testament and New Testament here at
the Seminary."

Nothing pleases me more than to hear students say and mean this. (Lessons in humility are harder to learn than the names of the Old Testament minor prophets.)

Alongside this student's experience with a well-informed church deacon I put my own experience last week while visiting a different kind of a church member in another parish: the Newport Methodist Church, where student Thomas Longstaff is serving. I found the lady parishioner less than excited about the Sunday sermons she tries to listen to, which, she explained, are "so larded with theological school language that most of the people snooze while he preaches."

This lady further informed me that she is nonplussed by the term "trinitarian." "The way our student talks," she said, "you can't be a Christian unless you *are* a trinitarian. Well, I'm a trinitarian all right, but of course I don't believe in the Holy Ghost."

The same day I visited the Plymouth parish, not far from Newport, and discovered a lady much dissatisfied with her student minister's Easter sermon. "I hoped," she reported, "that we were going to hear all about life in the hereafter; instead he talked about theology. I'm a Methodist. What I'm interested in is the gospel; I don't want to hear about theology."

All kinds of candidates for ministry come to Bangor Seminary. While they are students they go to all kinds of churches where they preach all kinds of sermons to all kinds of people.

Because of the endless variety I find in my work

with congregations I've come to dislike the phrase "the average church member." There's no such a person, any more than there's an average baby, or school teacher, or office janitor, or divinity student.

April 30

Fishing, golfing, and camping make lay people reluctant to help with the spring cleaning of church lawns and the painting of weather-beaten buildings. (Too, these good people have their own places to tidy up.) So, more than often, ministers are unable to enlist the aid of trustees and deacons for Saturday afternoon projects. Sometimes, though, they do get half-hearted promises to help beautify the church premises.

A week ago in the Seminary bookstore I overheard a conversation between two pastors who serve in the same community and whose churches are on opposite sides of the main street. One student commented to the other that at last he had "gotten one trustee to paint the church steps next Saturday afternoon." The other lad remarked that one of his deacons had agreed to set out evergreen trees on the church lawn.

The following Saturday afternoon, as the first student painted the church steps, he saw the other student setting out evergreens.

No trustee or deacon was anywhere in sight.

May 2

How to get people out to church. Dismayed by scanty attendance at Sunday worship, some student ministers resort to ingenious devices to entice people into pews.

One such student dropped into a chair in my office and described his campaign to increase attendance in the coastal church he is serving. He painted a bleak picture but was able to grin about it.

At a recent church meeting he prodded the congregation to elect a seven-member attendance committee. The job of the committee was to telephone, write to, or call upon non-attenders to spur them to occupy pews more often than on Easter. The results on the first Sunday following the campaign were both encouraging and distressing. Several members who had been lapsing in attendance reappeared at worship, but absent were all seven members of the attendance committee.

Another student serving a village church on Mount Desert Island put the following into his Sunday bulletin:

> On . . . too . . . many Sundays the . . . church looks like this . . . to . . . the pastor . . . as he looks over . . . the congregation . . . from the . . . pulpit. OnEasterthechurchlookslikethis.Let'skeepit thiswayeverySunday.

My own days as pastor of a church provided some humiliating moments. I remember how troubled I was when attendance at worship sagged. I found that many Sunday Stay-At-Homes were unconvinced that I or any minister could, in sermons, present a helpful or inspiring word, so they remained Stay-At-Homes. At a youth fellowship discussion one Sunday evening while I was a pastor, a teenager artlessly explained why her father never attended worship:

"He thinks he knows more than the preacher."

After a pause she added, "He does."

May 4

When I visit in Swanville I always enjoy a refreshing conversation with Ray Robertson. The tiny village church, loved by Ray, has been served by a long string of student ministers. (Ray, well along in years, can't remember when the church had a full-time minister.) He has worked with students when they asked his help, guided them when they requested his counsel, and been tolerantly amused when they took "wild swings" in their church work.

He's always compassionate when he evaluates the effectiveness of pastors, but frank, too. When he gives me his impressions of a minister he frequently comes up with a homely but telling analogy that describes some distinctive characteristic of the student.

Paul Willard, a Seminary junior, has been working hard with the handful of Swanville church people — that is, when he hasn't been working against them. He is considered by Ray and several members to be obstinate and bullheaded, although altogether likeable.

"That young man," Ray mused, "reminds me of a veal calf I once had. When he got his head down and had a destination in mind nothing on two feet could stop him. He was one hundred and fifty pounds of pure stubbornness."

"Has Paul been on any stiff-necked rampages lately?" I asked Ray.

"Indeed he has. The young fellow wants the church redecorated and knows exactly how it should be done, and he got his way over almost unanimous opposition. His determination is too much for us. He gets what he wants because he wears us down."

If Willard continues as persistent about his Christian principles, he should be able to provide a useful and forceful ministry.

Footnote: A graduate of the class of 1943, Frederick W. Whittaker, who became president of the Seminary, is one of the most stubborn people I've known. Through many of the years of his presidency he tried, with the assistance of the faculty, to secure accreditation for Bangor by the Association of Theological Schools. After several unsuccessful attempts the faculty gave up on the effort, mumbling that the president was chasing a mirage. Whittaker kept doggedly on: mapping new strategies, preparing self-studies, and bringing inspection teams to Bangor until the rest of us grew weary of being examined. We said, "Our particular approach to theological education will never win recognition." Back would come F.W.W. with another effort and behold, in 1974, he got what he was after: Bangor achieved accreditation — the fruit of stubbornness!

May 7

Now and then unpleasant dilemmas greet student pastors as soon as they get their feet down in Maine villages. Some people still seem to think that a minister — even a student minister — should know how to work the kinks out of his parishioners' lives.

A young pastor came to my office this morning irked by the criticism of both church people and others in the community for the role he played in the life of a man who was confronting the town with a vexing problem. The local school principal recently went on a bender for just about all of one school week. The school committee was sorely distressed, and deciding that the pastor of the village church might be of service, urged him to find the principal and rescue him. Except for an occasional lapse, the educator had been in good standing: popular with pupils and respected by parents. The school board agreed to reinstate him in their good graces if he would deny himself the bottle except during school vacations.

The enterprising pastor soon found the erring principal at home, and after a bit of moralizing, enthusiastically hauled twenty-five bottles — still full — to the town dump.

Several of the more straitlaced members of the congregation rebuked the student because he devoted so much time to the salvage mission, and one school committee member (whose brother is the manager of the local green front) disapproved of the minister's "altogether too energetic action."

The school principal was peeved because his liquor was confiscated.

May 8

One by one our campus elms are coming down. Every now and then I hear the snarl of a chain saw and looking out a window see another lofty but diseased tree crash to the ground. These trees in the past have not only beautified our hill but often, during the late spring, they have provided shade for outdoor classrooms where students and professors have talked informally.

Today under a remaining campus elm I had a long, agreeable conversation with a student who has been serving a church on Route 2 between Skowhegan and Farmington. Now a senior he will be receiving his diploma in a few days.

Well I remember how he looked when he first appeared on campus nearly five years ago: stocky, mustached, handsome, dressed in an almost complete cowboy costume — ten-gallon hat, neckerchief, wide, gem-studded belt, and high boots. I recall checking his folder — containing his application to enter the school, recommendations, and a short autobiographical sketch — to see whether he had really blown in from the western plains. I discovered he was thirty-nine years old and that his home had been on Long Island. I couldn't remember ever hearing of a Long Island cowboy.

After a year at Seminary he became minister in a Somerset County village. Almost immediately I received a phone call from a village church member who shouted, "What's the idea? This time you've saddled us with a phony cowboy."

"He's no phony," I objected, "merely dresses a little unconventionally." (At least he did not have hair to his shoulders or a full beard — hirsute adornments that arouse the vexation of some church people.)

"Well this guy comes from New York," I was hotly reminded, "not cattle country; tell him for us that if he wants to be useful around here, he's gotta get into some decent clothes right away."

After the phone call I sat down with the student and tried to interpret to him the puzzlement of the congregation about his garb. I tried to persuade him, since he was not being urged to back down on some religious conviction, to concede to the peoples' wishes and shuck his inappropriate costume. He came back at me fast: "Why should I? The way I dress has nothing to do with preaching the gospel. Nobody's going to dictate what I wear."

I mildly suggested to him that people were understandably mystified by his costume when they greeted him in the local grocery store, post office, and their homes. To avoid misunderstandings, why not wear more decorous apparel? I found him brittle on the matter. "I'm just not going to be told how to dress." And that was that.

The church people continued annoyed, but because the student was otherwise sensible and obviously a sincere Christian preacher, they learned to tolerate his uniform about town and even when he made pastoral calls. (One of his parishioners rather sarcastically reported to me that "at least the minister does manage to appear for Sunday worship by automobile, not by pony.")

Before the end of the first year in his parish I had another discussion with him and, although he made

130

no agreement to drop the cowboy motif, I noticed that he began to wear the same kind of jackets as other students on the campus. One after another he shed the offending garments; finally he appeared in a sport jacket and conservative slacks.

In these days just before graduation only the cowboy hat remains; and now he is ready to swap even that for a mortarboard.

May 10

Just after breakfast this morning as I was coming into the Seminary parking lot, two students waylaid me asking for a chance for one of them to supply the pulpit of a nearby church which right now has no settled minister. I had never before observed that either student was on fire to spread the gospel, and I was also aware that neither had a wife and children subsisting on crackers and sardines. So, I inquired why this sudden ambition to preach.

"We need the money," one insisted. As I hesitated the other explained: "Our roommate wants to paint the ceiling of the church he's serving; it's a mess. But he hasn't any money. We thought maybe you'd send one of us out to supply-preach for a Sunday. That way we might get fifteen or twenty dollars to buy the paint for him.

I decided I'd go along with the request; so, one will get the opportunity to preach, and the honorarium will be fifteen dollars. Thus, this church will serve a sister church — all unknowingly. A student will stand in the pulpit of one church to help paint the ceiling of another.

May 11

"All right to come in?" A young fellow of twenty-seven, Paul Clark, stood in my office doorway — tall, handsome, with searching eyes. I invited him to come in and sit down, but he could not seem to settle.

For four months he has been minister of the Clifton Baptist Church about fifteen miles from the campus. He has got on famously with the people in the church (his first), some of whom have been a little disillusioned with previous performances of part-time leaders.

"Please tell me about funeral services," he blurted, still on his feet. "I've never been to one; now I have to conduct one." I could feel his fear, fear that as pastor to a bereaved family he will fail to say the right words, and do the helpful thing.

His questions came in a shower: "Will the funeral director be sure to signal me when to begin the service? Do I stay with the family at the close of the service? Am I supposed to say anything personal about the person who has just died? How long should the service last? What do I do after I've pronounced the benediction, or is there a benediction at a funeral service?"

Of course I gave him what suggestions I could — understanding a little how he felt, remembering one fall day over thirty years ago when I was conducting the first funeral service I ever attended, recollecting my own near panic. After many more questions, he walked out of the office, looking preoccupied and somber; he never did sit down.

An afterthought crossed my mind. I realized I had said nothing to him about keeping in touch with the stricken family in the days following the funeral service.

May 12

All yesterday afternoon I had Clark on my mind; I wondered whether his anxiety had interfered with his keen desire to do and say the right things at the memorial service. This morning I searched for him, finding him in the Mail Room in Maine Hall. I asked him how he felt now that he had attended and conducted his first funeral service.

"I did the best I could. I'm going to see the family again in a day or two."

My mind was easy about Clark. The young man had the good sense to know his pastoral mission was incomplete unless he soon visited the bereaved. He has the makings of an excellent minister, and I hope he will find increasing fulfillment in his ministry.

I recalled another youthful minister who, a few years ago, got into real trouble conducting funeral services in the church he was serving in Waldo County. At the funerals of two prominent members of the community he read the Scripture and prayers, then made extended complimentary remarks about the lives they lived, ushering them through the Pearly Gates with a fanfare of trumpets and all flags flying. Soon after, the town "reprobate" died, and this time the student was at a loss for complimentary words. Said he to the people gathered for the service: *"If our brother had been a Christian and a practicing* church member, *if* he had loved the Lord, *if* he had made his peace with God, he *would have* gone to be with God."

The student left the brother there, obviously certain that the deceased was on his way to some other destination than Beulah Land.

Some time elapsed before he was invited to conduct another service in the town. Families of even "good-living people," and church members themselves, were uneasy as to how the young pastor might report on their loved ones at a memorial service.

May 13

It has been my experience that people in Maine churches have a pretty good supply of patience with student preachers' mistakes: mistakes in grammar, in pronunciation, in following the order of service from beginning to end, in reading announcements. Such blunders do not cancel the value of the service for those who attend worship.

Unfortunately, the Seminary chapel audience is far more critical. Often the minor blunders of visiting preachers destroy, in the minds of seminarians and their professors, the force of what could be an inspiring sermon.

This morning a visiting minister from a Waterville Baptist church was the leader of worship in the chapel. The response of many students was enthusiastic, but . . . No place can be found where the "but" habit is so liable to surface as when a clutch of preachers evaluate the sermon of another preacher.

Theological seminary professors are especially expert "butters."

"Sure, the visitor was a good preacher, but . . ." Then follows a detailed reservation as long as your arm about the sermon he preached. Often the whole sermon is spoiled for the scholarly members of the faculty if the preacher makes a mistake about some tiny particular. The preacher today had commanding delivery, logical order, stimulating thoughts, and a sound biblical base. "*But*, my soul, did you hear the date he gave to Tyndale's translation of the New Testament? Ruined the whole thing."

The helpful effect of the sermon got lost in a thicket of slavish attention to detail.

This afternoon, Howard Quirk, one of the most clever and witty divinity students I have known, and not lacking a generous supply of confidence in himself, met me on campus with a wry comment: "Humility is not often found in abundance at the Seminary, is it?"

Naturally I inquired what brought out this saucy remark and I got an even more saucy reply: "This morning after chapel I overheard comments by two of your colleagues about the guest preacher. The remarks were less than complimentary. I suppose every member of the faculty thinks himself to be the only really good preacher north of Union Seminary."

By biting my tongue I was able to refrain from giving Quirk a tidbit of information that would have pleased him mightily. In the morning mail I had received a letter from a Hancock County church to which I have been sending guest preachers for many

Sundays — this to continue until the church finds a full-time minister.

Up to now the church has been requesting three professors to every one student to supply its pulpit. If, as Quirk suggests, the professors are guilty of too much confidence in their own preaching strength, there is a message for them in the letter just received. The clerk of the church expressed the wishes of the congregation: "Please, up the quota of student supplies you are sending us, they are better preachers than the profs."

May 17

Among the letters my secretary left on my desk this morning was one from a tiny church in Piscataquis County. It was full of satisfied and glowing praises for the student minister's sermons, and was the kind of letter that helps to make my day.

A second letter, also from Piscataquis County, revealed a very *dis*satisfied customer; he just can't stand the preacher:

Dear friend Cook:

As you know, our house is right beside the church in our town. This morning early I heard a big racket over there and I told my wife to look out through the kitchen curtains to see what the preacher was doing. She looked, and said he seemed to be moving barrels around. "I guess he's putting out rubbish," she said.

This hit me hard — the bit about putting out rubbish. Friend Cook, that's what we get in this preacher's sermons — they're all rubbish. Can't you do something about this fellow? He's awful. Remember, you sent him to us . . .

136

The writer is a member of a church where for years, under the leadership of several pastors, the Sunday morning congregation has never numbered more than a dozen, even with acceptable preaching.

It is strange what triggers a letter. I wonder if this young minister had been more quiet about putting out his barrels of rubbish, would the writer ever have written about putting out sermons of rubbish?

May 18

What I had to listen to on the telephone this morning was far from pleasant. The call was from a member of the Princeton United Church of Christ. The student minister has just resigned and left Maine. On his way out of town, after his resignation, he dropped more than a hundred copies of a smart-aleck letter in the local Post Office addressed to Princeton people. The letter, sarcastic and spiteful, upbraided everyone for smugness and indifference to the church program.

The indiscriminate mailing included active and inactive church members and "outsiders" who have no interest in church affairs. After denouncing people who think they can worship God Sundays on the golf course, he wrote this paragraph:

"Why don't you stop fooling yourself? Medical science says that the mortality rate is still 100 percent. That means you're going to die. Maybe you think you'll be able to sneak past Saint Peter because you have been active in the Masons, or some service club. I doubt it. I suspect you'll end up in some place with a strong smell of brimstone."

Many loyal to the church are bewildered by the letter, justly feeling such treatment is undeserved. "Why didn't he give us the works while he was here?" the church member asked over the phone. "Then we could have discussed his discontent. Dumping the letters, then hightailing it out of town for good leaves us with no chance to defend ourselves. He's a coward!"

It's doubtful whether the Princeton church will accept another student as minister. I emphatically wish that all students could (1) resist the temptation to "tell 'em off" just as they leave a parish; (2) learn that nasty letters should be written in invisible ink and mailed in the parsonage woodstove.

May 20

A young, ambitious Seminary junior has been, for six months, pastor of a village church in Cumberland County, not far from Portland. The church plant when he became minister was in sad shape: plaster was falling off the walls of the sanctuary, gaping holes could be seen in the carpet, and several pews had become rickety and untrustworthy. (When people seated themselves after a hymn during Sunday worship the pews creaked alarmingly.)

The first Sunday he conducted services he discovered that the green plush chair behind the pulpit was not in prime condition either. During the prelude he sat down gingerly on the battered relic, quite sure that complete collapse was imminent. Right then the pastor determined "to do something about this;"

he made up his mind to get the church officials active in providing a remedy for the dilapidation all about.

It was not easy to galvanize the trustees into refurbishing projects. Nothing happened, except the plaster continued to fall, the tear in the carpet enlarged, and the pews still protested noisily. Although attendance at worship increased, members of the congregation were so accustomed to a poverty budget that they remained reluctant to undertake expensive repairs.

Finally the energetic young parson decided to take up an extra offering every Sunday until sufficient funds were on hand to at least begin renovating. The congregation was not jubilant about this technique, but because the pastor was faithful, hardworking, and generous himself, they consented to go along.

The extra offering was a success; a carpenter was hired, and repairs began. Carried away by the promise of achieving his goal, the zealous fellow took up a third offering during a service. After the service a parishioner commented: "All the preachers we've had talked about stewardship, but this one we've got here now thinks he's God's special businessman. It's getting so when you go to morning services you feel it's no pay no pray."

All the same, the offerings added up; tomorrow evening the congregation will dedicate a renovated santuary.

May 21

The village of Stonington has for me an enchantment all its own, and I'm always pleased when a Seminary student serves the Methodist church there; his presence provides an excuse for me to visit members of the parish.

Today, I drove from Bangor to Bucksport, through the Penobscots and Brooksvilles to Sargentville, then across the high bridge onto Deer Isle, across the causeway to the town of Deer Isle, and finally to Stonington.

What a highway! I'm sure it's one of the crookedest roads in Maine, especially when a motorist finds himself in the Brooksvilles. Some route numbers are so confusing that strangers drive round and round until, totally bewildered, they stop at one of the general stores to ask directions. But for me it's a grand trip always, and today under clear skies it was especially exciting with its distant vistas of Blue Hill and stunning prospects of ocean. The broad view from the top of Caterpillar Hill was almost as appealing as Stonington itself, which is set on a steep hillside looking as though the smallest tremor would slide it into the Atlantic.

Larry Zimmerman, student minister of the church, is one of the finest young ministers I know. He has served the church for six years — a long tenure for a student. Not only did I relish my visit to the village, but I delighted in the reports I got from the people of the parish about their parson's commitment and competence.

That young fellow is reliable, hard working, and imaginative — with just a touch of charisma.

May 23

What a pleasant drive I had this spring morning to Sebec Village where I conducted worship for a student who took the day off to bone up on his last final examination! The church is small, like the village in which it is set, but most pleasing in its fresh coat of white paint. Inside, the building has a tasteful red and white decor and is equipped with an unusually tuneful electric organ.

Only twelve were present at the morning service, three of whom sang harmoniously as a choir. Although no other church is open for Sunday morning services within at least ten miles, the members of the Sebec congregation are discouraged by the pitifully small attendance and may decide to close during the next winter.

Following the benediction, Dorothy Preble, a faithful and concerned member, lamented the absence of people she felt should attend worship. She commented that they had *such* a pretty church, a good though small choir, a hard-working ladies aide, and a little minister who was the salt of the earth.

After a pause she added, "All we need is a congregation."

May 24

This morning there was a telephone call from the Days Ferry Congregational Church in Woolwich that revealed I still have a lot to learn in guiding my class in preaching. Yesterday I sent a student to supply the Ferry church, hoping he would do so well that the congregation would call him to become its pastor.

The student is conscientious, earnest and anxious to succeed; he sat up late Saturday night going over the next day's sermon by reading it to his roommate. But according to this morning's telephone report from a member of the church pulpit committee, the student was a pathetic failure at the Ferry. Although able to organize material for sermons, it is plain that he cannot organize himself.

While preaching Sunday he could not find the third page of his sermon. He halted abruptly and tried to *ad lib* while fumbling about on the pulpit to discover the lost material. After floundering helplessly he finally quit altogether, and then conducted a feverish search for the missing page under the pulpit, in the big pulpit Bible, and on a nearby stand. He even scrambled back to the chair behind the pulpit and peered beneath. No page. In dispair he announced the closing hymn number and concluded the service with a benediction: "Now unto him that is able to keep you from falling, and present you faultless . . ."

After the service the befuddled parson found the sermon page on the floor of his automobile.

The telephone voice of the irate church member admonished me: "If these students have to *read* their sermons, for goodness sake teach 'em the value of paper clips."

May 25
    "Beware the man who meets you at the train."

John Meisner — minister, farmer, state legislator — of Dover-Foxcroft remarked to me that these words of warning were spoken by one of his seminary professors over fifty years ago to young ministers accepting the responsibility of their first parishes.

Meisner, now well over eighty, prudent, and discerning, told me this afternoon about the aches and pains of a dynamic and attractive young theological student who is serving a nearby church. When the student first arrived he was heartily received and royally dined by a family that has now turned unpleasantly critical of him. The family met him almost as he drove into town, fed, advised, protected, and idolized him — at first. When he finally had to reject some of their instructions, they cast him off. Now they do not even speak to him, and they worship at another church.

It is important for young ministers as they come new to parishes not to accept too readily donations, opinions, loans, and intimate disclosures of any one person or family in the church. Someone in almost every church meets an arriving minister at the "station," eager (perhaps unconsciously) to boss, smother, own, or guide him, especially if he is a student minister, young and personable. And single. An unmarried minister is doubly vulnerable to the managerial tendencies of aggressive church members who are sure they know what is best for the congregation and pastor.

(It is taken for granted by all pulpit committees that married parsons are always better able than single ones to find acceptance in their congregations. This is *not* always true, I think.)

All women from eighteen to eighty will forgive a single minister almost anything. When he bungles or makes a hash, they say, "There now, if he had a good wife he wouldn't blunder that way."

I've come to think that this is a clear case of identification on the part of the good ladies.

May 26

Dignity is not always the mark of student ministers, although many a time they make up in enterprise what they lack in grooming and propriety of dress.

The Machias Universalist Church, closed for several years, now has student pastor Walter Smith, who is casual in costume and manner. Recently a few church fathers were startled and a little disturbed to spot pastor Smith working at the local supermarket to add to his salary paid by the church. Stowing canned goods in paper bags and pushing grocery carriages to parked cars seems to them to be lacking in ministerial decorum. Smith, however, was not at all dismayed when the news reached him that his unconventional ways were shocking to some.

His second summer in Machias he became coach of the Machias Little League baseball team. Church folk now noticed with some disfavor that he had exchanged his supermarket apron for a Little League baseball cap and sweatshirt, which he wore all about the county seat with a jaunty air.

Emma Means, an influential Machias matriarch, out of step with the stuffier members of the congregation, refused to censure young Smith. "No matter what he's got on," Mrs. Means said, "he's doing more for Machias kids than anyone else has done for ten years."

The eyebrows of sedate church members rose higher when they heard that their pastor was impresario at teenage hop sessions on Saturday evenings. The report is that fifty to seventy youngsters attend these while Smith twangs a guitar.

The young parson has been capable of agile adaption. After a Saturday evening dance, he works on his sermon, then steps into the pulpit early Sunday morning with poise and assurance. People are pleased with his sermons; both content and delivery have been highly satisfactory, and Emma Means has been heard to remark that "as long as young Smith puts up a neatly packaged sermon on Sunday mornings he can package all the groceries he wants to during the week."

May 27

This afternoon I got a savage impulse to "let her have it" when a lady member of a Waldo County church complained to me about the inexperience of student ministers. Said she: "In this village we're sick and tired of enduring novice ministers from that Seminary. If only we could have someone with spiritual depth."

She is a member of a church potentially strong enough to support a full-time pastor; so, I just had to say, with perhaps more heat and stiffness than was called for, "Madame, rouse yourself, stir up interest among other church members, expand the church budget to provide a living wage for a college and seminary educated minister, and go get one."

Afterward I somewhat repented of my bruskness because Waldo County *has* "endured" its share of beginning parsons. Many of its churches are too small to even think of getting the services of an ordained minister; but by a substantial buildup in dedicated giving, a few churches might get the full-time leadership they long for.

Meanwhile the doors of these churches stay open for Sunday worship because men and women students from the Seminary are giving the best they have.

May 28

The student leader of one of the Dixmont churches has a lively sense of humor; he has need of it, especially when he tries to arrange "special" music for Sunday services. Today he described to me a problem in the music "department" of the church that might well discourage seasoned ministers of many years' service. Somehow he manages to see the comicality of a grim and depressing situation.

With a wide grin he told me about a maiden lady who is the organist for the junior choir. The lady, who is most gracious and dedicated, holds rehearsals at her home where she plays on an ancient and wheezy pump organ. (The air for the bellows is supplied by vigorously tramping on a pair of plaid-carpeted foot pedals.) The tyrannical mother and father of the organist have for years objected to junior choir youngsters tracking into the house for practice; so, the good lady has had to push the instrument to an opened window while the children gathered outside the window to rehearse next Sunday's anthem.

"Believe it or not," the student concluded, "this same procedure is followed during December, January, and February."

June 1

Student William Hamel has been striving to meet the needs of the church school at Dedham, where there are not enough rooms for the activities of children who have only the church auditorium for their classes.

The members of the ladies circle have been sympathetic, and told Hamel that they would try to stir the church people to raise money to renovate the church basement for classrooms. In their desire to help, the ladies hit upon the idea to start a Dedham Church Store.

They went to work, and secured the consent of Mr. and Mrs. Bert Doughty to establish a store on their front lawn. The store can now be seen on Highway 46 between East Holden and Dedham. The outlandish looking structure appears to be a shack, not a store. The ladies have filled it with needlework, rag dolls, cloth turtles, frogs, clowns, kittens, and rabbits. And outside, the whole lawn is cluttered beyond belief. Neighbors bring pots, kettles, fishing reels and rods, tires, stoves, ice boxes, bird cages, breakfast tables, ironing boards, window shades, buck saws, axe handles, bales of wire, driftwood, and battered picture frames. Junk, just junk! Yet, apparently, there's a bull market for junk, for last summer the store brought in over $1,400.

Often at breakfast the husbands of ladies circle members are reminded: "Don't you go by any town dump today without stopping." Half of the goods up for sale in the church store have been salvaged from dumps. One husband tugged home a battered hope chest that sold for fifteen dollars. Another husband brought back two kitchen chairs covered with hen manure. After being washed by heavy rains, the chairs were sold to a vacationing out-of-state motorist who refinished them and stopped by the store the following summer to gloat: "Wish you could see my beautiful chairs now."

The ladies, with the help of their husbands, sons, and neighbors, pursued the enterprise with such earnestness that soon their savings bank passbook showed enough of a balance to begin work on the needed classrooms.

Last week Mrs. Doughty stood on her porch with me and surveyed the welter of gleanings from the dumps of Dedham, Holden, Clifton, Eddington, North Ellsworth, and elsewhere. Said she: "My house and yard have been a mess ever since we started the store, but I've been awfully happy."

Mr. Doughty grunted, "At least I don't have to mow the lawn."

June 2

In looking over the list of churches served by students I was startled this morning to find twelve of

148

the parishes have no connection with any denomination. Such churches are usually made up of religious people who come together on Sunday morning for a "meeting." They don't "belong" to that particular church but hold membership in churches in other towns where they once lived.

The Community Church in Canaan is a good example. About twenty attend Sunday worship and come from many denominations: Nazarene, Baptist, Seventh Day Adventist, Methodist, Congregationalist, Episcopalian, Friends Meeting, Presbyterian, Christian Scientist. No Muslims.

The Canaan congregation has remained steadfast in its resistance to becoming affiliated with any denomination.

Recently the members accepted a student to be their minister. After two Sundays the student came by my office to say, "This church I've been called to serve ought to be connected with some denomination." I agreed in principle but cautioned him to move in that direction with the greatest restraint.

After several weeks I decided to go to Canaan which is fairly new to the Seminary as a student charge. I found out a great deal more about the congregation than that they were reluctant to affiliate with any denomination. I called first on the chairperson of the pulpit committee and began inquiring whether their new student pastor was making an effective start and whether he was well received by the people. The chairperson was very blunt about the student:

"He's a radical!"

"What do you mean? How is he radical?"

"Well, he wants to organize our church."

"Surely you already have an organization."

"Of course we have. We've got a flower committee, a music committee, a pulpit committee, two deaconesses, and four deacons."

"Have you noticed any other radical ideas of your student minister?" I wanted to learn all I could.

"We certainly have. He thinks we ought to join up with some denomination. But we're dead set against that. We're independent and we're going to stay just that: independent!"

I can't say I'm wholly out of sympathy with the chairperson's stance. Taking into account the different church backgrounds of those who attend meetings, I cannot imagine *which* denomination would be suitable to all. And, in these days when church union and interdenominational cooperation are stressed, it seems as though the Canaan church is already engaged in its own brand of ecumenicity.

June 3

Making pastoral calls on members of congregations is burdensome to some young church leaders who are often at a loss for "something to say." One shy beginning pastor confessed to me that when he attempted his first pastoral visit, he rang the doorbell of the parishioner's home, waited a moment, and then ran down the road before the bell was answered. Another shrinking violet admitted that at first when he rang a doorbell, he half-hoped nobody would answer.

Others, however, go everywhere with ease and find visiting everybody heartwarming and even exciting.

Visiting parishioners of course is not as glamorous for pastors as preaching sermons. After a minister has delivered an inspiring or searching sermon, the hearers sometimes remark, as they go out the church door: "That was a great message, Reverend." But only seldom does a minister receive vocal commendation for making a neighborly call. As the pastor goes out the door of a home after a visit with the family, he is not speeded on his way with a remark like, "that was a great pastoral call, Reverend." Never.

Yet some students delight in wearing out shoe leather and car tires in the business of getting into peoples' homes. A couple of weeks ago I talked with a junior who is awakening new interest in a Washington County Congregational church he has been serving. I asked him how he was getting such an enthusiastic response: "Why are you attracting a larger attendance than any recent pastor before you?"

With a grin he readily acknowledged, "It's sure not because I'm a terrific preacher."

When I talked with his church members I found it was because he knows them as friends and is interested in everything about them. They said, "He's always dropping in for a few minutes on somebody. He knows *us;* we know *him.*"

One church member told me that this young pastor was recently invited to supper at a home noted for clutter, untidiness, and dirt. Still he went, showing not one whit of disdain for the unkempt surroundings. No wonder the community appreciates him.

June 7

Right after lunch today I drove the Moosehead Trail (Route 7) to Jackson; there I talked with a devoted member of the Congregational Church now without a student minister. She described the difficulties she and a handful of others meet in "keeping open" the tiny village church:

"Only a scattering of people support our church; if only more would attend and work, we could have a solid church in town." She expressed, too, a longing for spirited leadership. "I remember," she mused, "once when I went to Belfast to see a movie about Peter Marshall. Now, if we could only get a minister like that, or half as good, or even a *quarter* as good, we'd have a flourishing church."

Inwardly I thought, "If only you could rally the people of this village behind the student I'm sending to you, or half the people, or even a *quarter* of the people you might help to *make* a Peter Marshall." For often I see how much faithful lay people can do to help a pastor. When a student learns he can count always on the labor, friendship, counsel, and prayers of a dozen staunch church members he can become a real power for God.

June 8

"If all the students and professors who go to sleep in chapel were laid end to end in the pews we'd be a lot more comfortable."

I overheard this sarcastic remark by a seminarian

152

after an unusually dull sermon delivered in the chapel by a visiting bigwig preacher who put just about all of us to sleep.

Well, perhaps the students who listened, or half-listened, received some negative guidance on how *not* to preach. Students listening and observing can learn much from veterans of the pulpit: what to say and what not to say, what will keep people awake and what will put them to sleep. So, I often admonish my class in preaching to grasp every opportunity to listen to seasoned speakers.

This afternoon Robert Sargent, student minister of a Congregational church in Washington County, told me how much *he* had learned from watching the "experienced" minister of another church in town. The latter preached the baccalaureate sermon for the senior class of the neighborhood high school, and excitedly pictured the grim world of hopelessness into which the seniors would be going. "The world is running to three evils," he declaimed, "alcoholism, sex, and socialism," coming down particularly hard on the last of the three.

A man in the audience became restless and obviously disgusted; his face seemed to show powerful distaste for the minister's message. He appeared to be thinking, "This preacher is surely sending these young people out into despair." Finally, the indignant listener grasped the back of the seat in front of him, pulled himself up, and shouted, "I protest." The preacher, at a moment's loss, recovered and said, "I have a perfect right to speak as I see fit." "You're going too far," the man protested. Still the minister continued in a negative vein; after a while the objector exercised *his* perfect right to get up and walk out.

Young Sargent said to me, "That whole business taught me something. I'll try to put at least a few words of hope into every sermon I preach."

June 11

New Sharon has enjoyed the services of several resourceful student ministers, none more than the present one, Bob Dobson, who employed a unique method of recruiting teachers for the Federated Church's summer daily vacation Bible school.

As in all parishes, getting a staff for a school is a big problem: fathers are at their jobs, mothers are out working too, or busy at home. Bob wanted to enlist the help of one particular mother, who he knew would make a fine teacher but had many children to scrub, clothe, and feed. "I'd like to help," she declared, "but I'd better not do it. I need to be home all summer; my house is a mess and I have to clean it; I'm sick of living in a heap." The minister quickly promised, "My wife and I will help you clean a couple of afternoons a week if you'll teach."

He meant it, too. After the morning Bible school classes were over he pushed a vacuum cleaner, washed windows, and entertained the teacher's children, while his wife swept, ironed, and mopped.

June 13

Herbert Moore, rough and ready student pastor of the Kenduskeag Union Church, believes in visiting everybody in town: non-church goers as well as members. He calls hopefully upon prospects he wants to interest in the church. Last week he knocked at the door of a stranger to the church and got a surprise. The man who opened the door did not know Moore, and briskly asked the parson, "What's on your mind?"

Herb said, "I'm the new minister of the village church."

Before the preacher could say more, the man turned his back. "Sarah," he yelled, "it's for you," then vanished through a door leading to the cellar.

Student ministers in small churches often say, "In the church I serve, religion is for women only." Of course, men do attend worship, but it does seem as though one Seminary senior hit it right when, after two years of work in the Moosehead Lake country, he said, "The men in Maine towns use their snowshoes and snowmobiles in winter, their fishing rods in spring, their golf clubs in summer; and in the fall they use Sundays to rest up from the exertions of the other three seasons."

The Bangor senior is not the first pastor who has felt that Sundays mean church for women, sports for men.

It wasn't too many years ago that Ralph Waterhouse, student leader of the church at Weld, stopped me on the campus for a chat. He was always reporting to me some uncommon event in his small church. I could often tell before he spoke, by the expression on his face whether the happening was good or bad. That morning I was greeted by a wide smile. "What do you know!" he announced, "I had a man in church yesterday!"

June 15

"Every time a new student comes to our church," reports a member of a Penobscot Valley congregation, "we get a change in the order of the service, in the by-laws (or several new ones added to the old set), in the Sunday school lesson material, in the minister's pulpit clothing, and in just how many minutes before the Sunday service the steeple bell should be rung."

Such changes made abruptly at the time a new student arrives with new ideas are frequently disconcerting to congregations. Some churches have been served so many years by students that members become reluctantly expectant of alterations each time a new one arrives. (A member of the pulpit committee of Bangor's Forest Avenue Congregational Church told me that so far as he knows, that congregation has been served by students for sixty-five years. With different students following one another every two to four years the worshipers have surely suffered jolting confusions.)

The latest "change" I heard about had to do with a student preacher's platform stance while delivering his sermon. This young man stopped me in the vestibule of the chapel yesterday to say that he preached last Sunday's sermon sitting down.

"Why?" I wanted to know. "Were you tired or did you lose your footing?"

"Oh no," he said, and added earnestly: "I wanted to create an atmosphere of informality in the service, so I pulled up the big platform chair beside the pulpit, sat down, and just talked to the people. It was a kind of fireside chat, and it was so effective I plan to do it again."

I just looked at him, and said nothing.

After a moment he volunteered that he had Biblical support for his unconventional gimmick: "You know," he said, "Jesus preached that way; he sat on a mountain top and talked to people. He also did it from a boat and while sitting in the temple." He whipped out three texts (Matthew 5:11, Mark 4:1, Matthew 26:23) to prove his point, and looked entirely satisfied with himself.

I speculated on what members of the congregation might think about their sitting down preacher, and resolved to visit them soon to discover — among other things — whether such casual performances obtain in other areas of his work.

This morning's mail brought a message for me and for him. A member of the church wrote that he and several others of the congregation are less than enchanted by the stripling preacher's pulpit posture. "Was he sick?" the writer asked. "I didn't get a chance to speak with him after the service. Or was he just trying to be folksy and informal?"

June 17

Because of the severe limits on their time, parish calling is not easy for students to fit into their schedules. The young fellow who is in the Hancock Congregational Church believes in informing his congregation that he *is* finding time to fulfill this part of his mission.

In a low-keyed way he advertises the calls he makes. When he visits a "shut-in" he tells her of the wonderful visit he has just enjoyed with an old friend of hers,

157

and that yesterday he called at the hospital in Ellsworth on a previous sexton of the church whom she has known for years. This is not only good strategy, but gives him an opportunity to report on the welfare of old friends to one another.

Another young man serving a parish in Kennebec County has not been as resourceful or faithful a visitor. Several times he has failed to call at homes where there has been serious illness or to seek out members in some kind of distress.

Not long ago Billy Hatch, a member of the church, had the shingles. The pastor, because of preoccupation with lesser things, failed to visit the man at home. A few months later, Billy, in trouble again, went to the hospital for a gall bladder operation; this time the pastor arrived in the ward with a cordial hand extended and a cheerful, "How are you doing, Billy?"

Weeks later after Billy was up and about, and still smarting from the parson's neglect, he said to the village storekeeper, "What d'yer know, the preacher called on me when I was in the hospital. He had his nerve calling me 'Billy'; why, he'd never even seen me before."

"Not even last Easter, Billy?" inquired the storekeeper.

June 19

Who owns the church?

Many times I have encountered some church member who takes for granted that he owns it. He behaves as though the deed for the building is locked up in his own safety-deposit box. I know a church

158

treasurer who has held that position for fifteen years and seems to think the congregation's bank account belongs to him. I'm also acquainted with a certain church "boss" who operates as though the entire organization is his special fief. Just the other day I talked with a rich widow who, in the role of Lady Bountiful, is the largest contributor to a church in Franklin County; other members do not dare to go against her wishes for fear of losing her well-stuffed offering envelopes. People in the community refer to the church as "her" church.

Then, too, there's the ladies circle *collective* ownership of the church building. "Nothing can be done about the plumbing in the basement," moans a trustee, "without the backing of the members of the Busy Helpers Woman's Society."

Churches with a numerous membership are less prone to be "owned" or bossed by one person or group, but the possessive spirit of some members easily besets congregations with only a handful of workers. And, I've never known any one member to "own" a church unless other members sit back, mum and glowering, and *let* him take over. Student ministers confronted by this ownership problem often seek to stir lackluster, indifferent members to active leadership.

While visiting in West Bethel I heard an outlandish tale about how, many years ago, the ownership of the village church was established. A certain businessman in the hamlet grew rich through shrewd investment. As years passed he became apprehensive about his account in the heavenly economy; so, he decided to be on the safe side by providing for the pious folk in the community a beautiful lot on which to build a meeting house. To doubly insure his safe passage into glory he also supplied all the construction material for an edifice.

The building was soon erected, and the first of a long line of student ministers began work in the town. The religious zeal of the benefactor did not involve attendance at Sunday worship; he felt that by donating land and lumber he now had gilt-edge holdings on the "other shore."

A young parson, newly arrived in town and out making calls, met the philanthropist on the road, and after passing the time of day inquired, "Do you belong to the church in town?"

"No," Moneybags replied, "the church belongs to me."

June 26

"After observing a student serve his first parish, can you tell whether he is on his way to becoming a useful minister?"

So often members of churches I visit ask this question. The answer is no, I can't tell. But I do get at least an inkling about his future ministry. If when a church does not flourish — its members do not attend worship faithfully, nor contribute generously, nor serve willingly as officers and on committees — and the student pastor can still keep a spirit of hopefulness and a sense of humor, he will not only survive as a minister, he will achieve much for the Lord.

Edgar Jones is a good example of a student minister who keeps his sense of humor. Over coffee this morning he described several melancholy weekend encounters in his church work. Jones works hard to bring people to Sunday services in the Phillips United Church of Christ and is getting a favorable response. But despite his helpful preaching and faithful parish visiting, attendance at worship has picked up only slowly.

Last weekend Jones made ten visits and ran into the following threadbare excuses for non-attendance at worship by hardened Sit-At-Homes:

"Sunday's the only day in the week I can sleep in."

"I don't have to go to church to be a Christian."

"If I go to hell for not coming to church, at least I'll have plenty of company."

"I worship God on Sunday when I go fishing up at Rangeley."

"Of *course* I believe there ought to be a church open in town; and even if I don't ever attend, my heart is with you."

Said Jones with a grin, "Once in a while one of these members shows up in church — once in a *great* while." He added jokingly that he is thinking of keeping a couple of spare blockbuster sermons under the pulpit Bible that he can pull out and deliver when one of these delinquents happens to appear at worship (probably on a Sunday when the member's little daughter is up front to "speak a piece" at the children's day exercises). These would be very special sermons, pointed sermons, said Jones, that "I wouldn't think of preaching to the people who are almost always present."

At Seminary, Jones is a Canteen Room radical. Coke in hand, surrounded by other students, he sounds for all the world like a dedicated reformer: valiant, prophetic, a foe of every injustice. In Phillips he is cautious and subdued.

Some young preachers are prudent enough to know where to blow off steam without risking the loss of their pulpits.

June 29

About noon a few days ago, as I came out of an Ellsworth bakery carrying a half-dozen of my favorite raisin buns in a paper sack, I saw a member of the Dennysville Congregational Church sitting under a big elm near the bakery pouring coffee into a Thermos bottle cap. He invited me to sit down and share his coffee. After I got comfortable I presented him with a bun. Then I made a big mistake: I asked him whether the student minister in his town was usefully investing his summer in church work. Alas, he had a beef as long as his arm about the pastor's lack of care of the parsonage lawn.

"It's a disgrace," he grumbled. "Here it is the last of June and the guy hasn't mowed it yet. Looks like a hayfield."

This was my day off and I should not have asked even a casual question. Right then I was not interested in probing further into the preacher's activities — or lack of them. What I wanted to find out was whether my lunching companion had enjoyed any luck fly-casting on the Dennys River. My question about his minister sure opened a can of worms. But anyhow, before I got him around to a discussion of fishing, I made a mental note to see what I could do to nudge student Hans Schilling, who not incidentally weighs 309 pounds, into mowing that parsonage lawn.

Later when I talked with Hans about his care of the parsonage premises he readily confirmed that he had been slack, but said that the steep pitch of the sweeping lawn had discouraged him. I urged him to get active on the project.

Today when I visited the parish I found he had done his job — or overdone it. He had scoured about all of eastern Washington County until he found a huge grass mower with a sturdy seat. The crushing bulk of the minister had helped cut the grass very close. A church member passing the manse told me he had slowed to watch the operation and commented, "It was hard to tell whether the preacher was mowing the lawn or plowing the yard."

June 30

While in Dennysville yesterday I picked up the story of how student Schilling got the church steeple painted. (I had been noticing on visits to the community that the structure supporting the spire needed attention.)

Hans has felt that getting that steeple painted was as important as preaching sermons and far more important than plugging at his New Testament Greek. But when he broached the matter to the church treasurer he discovered no balance existed in the bank account to finance the undertaking; moreover the congregation was reluctant to engage right then in any

163

big project. Nevertheless the pastor called a business meeting hoping to overcome the reluctance.

"There's no money and it would cost several hundred dollars," volunteered one foot-dragger.

Schilling said, "Let's *raise* some money. We'll have a chicken barbecue, and invite people from all the villages around." The response was lukewarm, so Schilling put on the barbecue practically by himself and raised all the money needed.

The church people continued indifferent or irresolute on the paint job, so Hans called another meeting for further discussion. Several members were doubtful whether the steeple was sturdy enough to support scaffolding.

Schilling said, "I'm sure it will. The other day I climbed around on the beams up there, and I'll be glad to work on it myself.

Beholding the 309-pound steeple-jack willing to risk his life, the objectors became silent and the steeple got painted.

July 1

In coming years churches in Maine that are served by students will be treated to many tradition-breaking programs. I hope that valid traditions will not be replaced by fads, notions, whims, and wrong-headed experiments. Some changes that have taken place in the last few years seem contrived and just pasted on.

Student ministers may be counted on to alter worship patterns, set up new forms of administration, modify pastoral goals and inaugurate novel Christian education programs. But to make the right changes, to the right degree, and in the right way — this they will find difficult.

Many elderly church members are not taking kindly to recent innovations. Some are puzzled and some are "put out" with students who replace a pipe organ with a guitar, a pulpit gown with a yellow turtle neck sweater, bread and grape juice in communion with cheese bits and tea, hymns with folk tunes.

"The next thing our pastor will want," said a trustee of the Winthrop United Church of Christ, "is bucket pews."